M000211406

In *The Code of Behavior*, Jason L. Nemes demystifies the secret of success. His practical book reveals that when we change our code, we can change our lives. Better yet, he shows us how with five essential steps.

—Chris Robinson
Executive Vice President, Maxwell Leadership

Jason's life is what dreams are made of. Understanding the need to change, reflect, and believe in yourself to achieve your goals despite the odds is what this book brings to you. In *The Code of Behavior*, Jason guides you through this code to make you believe in yourself. If you are looking for a change, this book is it.

—David Chen
Investor of Faze Clan, managing partner of GTIF Capital, and president of North American Collegiate League

Jason lives and breathes his code of behavior. It's a part of who he is and what he wishes for others. Reading this book can change your life, provided you take positive action to be the best you can be personally and professionally. Jason will inspire you to set high goals and then reach even higher. He believes in you. All you need to do is believe in *yourself*.

—Mark Lachance
CEO of Maxy Media, and author of
Wall Street Journal and *USA Today*
Bestseller *The Lucky Formula*

THE CODE OF BEHAVIOR

5 ESSENTIALS TO UNLOCKING A LIFE OF EXTREME INSPIRATION, UNLIMITED CONFIDENCE, AND ENDLESS VICTORY

JASON L. NEMES

ethos
collective

Published by Ethos Collective
P. O. Box 43, Powell, OH 43065
www.EthosCollective.vip
All rights reserved.

LCCN: 2022904604

ISBN: 978-1-63680-070-7 (paperback)
ISBN: 978-1-63680-071-4 (hardback)
ISBN: 978-1-63680-072-1 (e-book)

Available in paperback, hardback, e-book, and audiobook.

ACKNOWLEDGMENTS

To God and to my mother Leslie Batten, father Michael Nemes, stepfather Patrick Batten, grandmother Susie Brant, sister Arielle Nemes, girlfriend Ana Avila, friend Mark Lachance, and all the people who have helped me on my journey—thank you!

DEDICATION

Jacob,

I love you and miss you, little bro.

CONTENTS

FOREWORD

Jason Nemes is one of those guys who draws people in like a magnet.

To be fair, his appearance commands attention. He's got more tattoos than I can count.

And his physique—seriously, this man works hard at chiseling his body into shape.

All those things make people look his way, but it's not his appearance that pulls people in. It's his heart.

Jason's driving motivator in life is his heart for helping people become the best versions of themselves. He wants to see others succeed. He wants to inspire people to see past who they are now—beyond their challenges and self-imposed limitations—to the people they could become.

We met through a friend, bestselling author Mark Lachance. I knew from the first time we talked that Jason had something special to offer. And the thing is, Jason knows that, too, and he isn't afraid to tell you that he is destined for big things.

He is confident that he is—just like you are—meant for greatness.

From my vantage point, Jason is already doing pretty great. He is a successful business owner, a powerful speaker, and now an author. Jason has experienced life at the bottom of the ladder but chooses to climb to new heights every day. He does that by encouraging others to reach for the next rung on *their* ladders. That's his heart.

Here's the scary thing: One year before this book was released, Jason's heart stopped. Literally.

You'll read more about that experience in the next few pages, but I have to say that I am so glad that God spared Jason's life that Easter Sunday in 2021. Beyond the fact that I wouldn't have had the pleasure of getting to know him, I'm thankful that God made Jason's heart beat again because now he gets to share his heart and the life-changing message in *The Code of Behavior* with you.

I hope you're ready for what's coming because if you apply what you learn from this book, I know it can accelerate your own journey to greatness. We've each got a limited number of days on this planet, and not everyone is lucky enough to get an extension. If you know you want more out of life, now is the time to start. And *The Code of Behavior* shows you how.

—Kary Oberbrunner
Wall Street Journal and *USA Today* bestselling author

A NOTE TO THE READER

If you're in a place in your life where you feel like things are going pretty good—or even just okay, but you *know* there's more to life than the daily grind you're stuck in—you're in the right place.

Or maybe you're in a place in your life where you feel like you've messed up, failed, or made too many mistakes. I've got a message for you: You're in the right place too.

No matter what your life has been like up to now, right here, right now, reading this book is exactly where you need to be. You have the gift of this moment to decide that you want to turn things around and start living life with purpose. The second you make that choice and take the first step toward greatness, *everything* changes. Will your life turn around overnight? No. Just like working out one day won't change your physique and eating healthy one day won't have you drop the weight you're looking to lose, things don't happen overnight. One day, though, after you've taken enough of those steps in succession, you'll wake up *amazed* at where you are and how far you've come.

No one is destined for average. Average (or worse) is just the default mode we slip into when we take life as it comes instead of taking control and making it what it was meant to be all along. Here's the thing: Life isn't always what you expect, but it is what you make of it. You have the choice to allow that default mode to destroy your dreams or to make your dreams a reality. Either way, you choose.

You picked up this book, so *clearly* you're ready to move your life in a new direction—one filled with extreme inspiration, unlimited confidence, and endless victory. To get there, we're going to start simple because success *is* simple. In fact, it's as simple as ABC.

A = Assess Your Current Code of Behavior

Before you can get where you want to go, you have to understand where you are. So, first things first, I invite you to take the Successful Code of Behavior Assessment at TheCodeOfBehavior.com. It will be the first thing you see on the screen, and it is your key to understanding your starting point on this journey.

B = Believe That You *Can* Experience a GREAT Life

The Code of Behavior, above all else, is about mindset. It's about changing how you think because it's your mindset that has the biggest impact on your success in every part of your life. Belief is *powerful* and essential to your ability to create a great life. That's why throughout this book—as well as in my speaking engagements and my virtual and one-on-one coaching programs—my goal is to instill in you the belief that *you* have control over the life you experience. Your belief changes *everything*.

C = Create *Your* Code of Behavior

Information is only as good as the outcomes it produces. The essentials in this book work if you work. If you read this book without applying what you learn, you'll still be getting the same results that you're getting now. That's why at the end of every chapter, I'm giving you space to immediately reflect your personal code of behavior—your existing one and the one that will move you forward in life. *Please* be intentional about creating a code of behavior that serves you well. It will be the thing that moves you into *your* best life.

Too many people complicate success. They overthink things, get overwhelmed, and remain paralyzed—stuck in average. Let today be the day that you choose to shake off average and break free from whatever has been holding you back. Take the first step—and then the next. Keep going, one foot in front of the other, toward *your* greatness. This book and *your* code of behavior make it simple.

I know you're ready, so let's get started.

Chapter 1
THE DAY I DIED

Every man dies. Not every man really lives.

—**William Wallace**, Braveheart

APRIL 4, 2021, was a beautiful day in Austin, Texas. Enjoying the spring weather and taking it easy with friends and the woman I loved seemed like the perfect way to spend the holiday.

That's how I had planned to spend the day anyway.

What actually happened changed my plans—and almost took my life.

I started the day with a workout at Lifetime Fitness with my girlfriend, Ana. Afterward, she went with me to the basketball courts downstairs to watch me play basketball with some friends. I didn't *want* to play. Cardio wasn't a part of my workout plan, and, at 243 pounds, I was out of shape. My friends needed me for a three-on-three game, though, so even though I didn't feel like playing and knew I was risking rolling an ankle in my low-top shoes, I played. We worked up a sweat three games back-to-back.

When the last game ended, Ana and I headed to the car. We were walking through the parking lot when she asked, "Are you feeling okay?"

"Yeah," I said. "Why?"

"You just looked a little off your game out there," she said.

I'd felt fine on the court, a little tired, but I assumed it was because of the extra weight I was carrying and because I hadn't been doing cardio. Walking to the car, I still couldn't catch my breath. Her words were still hanging in the air when I felt a dull ache in my chest, and my arm started tingling like it had gone numb. I stretched my arm and hand a little, trying to work out the tingling.

Sometimes my bodybuilding days catch up with me. I've got a pinched nerve in my neck, so every once in a while, my arm goes numb.

It'll pass, I thought as I got in the car and concentrated on getting my breath back to normal.

We got on the highway and headed home. Rather than passing quickly, the pain in my chest intensified, and no matter how I shifted in my seat, I couldn't get the sensation in my arm to ease up.

Then my head started pounding.

I exited the highway and pulled into a gas station to get some ibuprofen and water to see if that would help with the pain. Instead of getting better, the pain just got worse, and I still couldn't catch my breath.

That's when Ana asked the question I hadn't thought to consider, "Does it feel like the first time you had a heart attack?"

My immediate response was "no," but when I stopped to think about it, I realized she was right. I don't know why I hadn't thought of that, except for that everything had seemed fine with my heart for the past year. Her question made me think of the chest pains that had eventually led a surgeon to put a stent in my heart 366 days earlier.

"Actually, yeah, it does. But last time, the pain went away quick, like in sixty seconds or less. This time it's getting worse," I said. "I think I want to go to an ER clinic. Just to be sure..." My heart and I had a history, and I wanted to make sure things were okay.

"Well, let's go," Ana said.

I searched my phone for the nearest emergency care clinic, which turned out to be only a mile or so away. In Austin traffic, it can take a half hour to go a few blocks, but it was Easter. Thank God. Between the holiday and the pandemic, the roads were empty. It only took about five minutes to get to the clinic.

I got out of the car, wincing at the pain in my chest and head and still struggling to normalize my breathing. My arms and legs worked fine, but they felt a little heavier than usual as I walked from the car, through the clinic doors, and to the front desk.

"Hello, sir, how can we help you?" asked the masked girl behind the desk. "I think I'm having a heart attack," I replied.

"Can I see your ID?"

Seriously? I'm having a heart attack! Who cares about IDs? That's what I wanted to say. Instead, when I patted my pocket and realized I'd left it in the car, I went *back outside* to get it. I had asked Ana to go on home and check on my dog and told her I'd call her to let her know what the doctor said. Thankfully, she hadn't left. When I went out to get my wallet, she handed it to me through the open window. (She told me later that she wasn't about to leave me there alone until she knew I was 100 percent okay.)

3

I went back inside and gave my driver's license to the woman at the desk.

The ID combined with the words *heart attack* were enough to get people moving. Skipping the typical paperwork, a nurse rushed me to a room and had me lie down on a bed where she quickly attached EKG leads to my chest.

The doctor took one look at the screen and said, "Sir, I'm sorry to tell you this, but you're suffering a severe heart attack."

No problem. I've already had one. That's the thought that ran through my head—*no big deal.* About eighteen months earlier, I'd had a heart attack and later had a stent put in, so I assumed that I would be walking out later that day. My body could handle another heart attack. Right?

Wrong.

The nurse had given me a couple of aspirins to chew, and after lying there for twenty or thirty minutes, I started to feel a little better. *Everything's gonna be fine* was what I thought right before I realized I was about to die.

One second I was thinking *no big deal*, and the next, darkness started to close in all around me. I knew I was dying.

"I feel myself about to fade out. Y'all gotta do something. Please help me. God, please help me." I barely got the words out before the blackness overtook me. It was a plea to the nurse who was standing next to me. More than that, it was a plea for supernatural help.

I don't remember what happened next. I don't remember the nurse standing over me, praying as she pounded my chest with rhythmic compressions to keep my blood flowing. I don't remember her yelling as she called the doctor back to the room. I don't remember the chaos that surely ensued as they got the crash cart and defibrillator ready.

I don't remember any of that because I was dead.

When I coded (which is what doctors call it when a person flatlines and needs resuscitation), the nurse, Debbie, performed CPR while the doctor hooked up the defibrillator, stopping only when he shouted, "Clear!"

The electric shock coursed through my body.

Forty seconds after my heart stopped, that jolt combined with the CPR brought me back to life.

I will never forget that moment of reawakening. *Did I make it?* I wondered. *Am I alive? If I'm not alive, please let me be in heaven!*

I couldn't open my eyes or move my body, but I heard the doctor say, "Jason, welcome back."

His voice told me I was alive, but I couldn't move. All around me, I could hear people talking and equipment moving. The paramedics had arrived at the clinic to transfer me to the hospital. I wanted to see what was going on, but all I could do was lie there.

In the darkness, I heard the doctor comment, "Jason, she just saved your life."

Thank you, God.

Warning Signs

Roughly eighteen months before that Easter Sunday, I was walking through the Denver airport after speaking at a leadership conference when a sharp pain in my chest stopped me in my tracks. It lasted forty-five to sixty seconds, and then it was gone just as suddenly as it had hit me. I didn't think much of it and continued to my gate, feeling a little out of breath.

What I didn't know then was that pain was my first heart attack.

Feeling strong and healthy is important to me, so when I got back home to Nashville, I joined the Orangetheory®

fitness center that was next door to my apartment building. I was in decent shape at the time, but I got a membership thinking that it wouldn't hurt to improve my cardio health. I also got back into boxing. I had been boxing for years, but I was new to Nashville and needed a place to train. I found a coach and new gym, picked up gloves, and got to work.

My chest ached every time I ran at the gym. I tried to push through it but would have to stop. In the boxing ring, it was the same story. After just a few minutes of training, I had nothing in the tank. I couldn't breathe and would have to stop. Exhausted, my arms and legs felt like lead. Having to tell the coach I needed to take a break really messed with my head. I was young and used to feeling invincible. Standing in the ring feeling weak and out of breath, I worried that the coach would think I was quitting because I was just tired or lazy—that I didn't want to keep working. The truth was I *couldn't* keep going because I literally couldn't breathe! I knew what being out of shape felt like, and this felt different—something wasn't right. Unable to ignore the warning signs any longer, I made an appointment to see a cardiologist at Vanderbilt University Medical Center.

The doctor ran a bunch of tests, including an ultrasound and echo cardiogram, and all the results showed that I was in perfect health. When I asked for a stress test, the doc shook his head. "Are you sure that you want to do a stress test? I really don't think you need one," he said. "Your ultrasound and EKG at rest are perfect. You're clearly in great shape."

I couldn't shake off the feeling that something wasn't right with my heart and finally convinced him to give me a stress test since the only time I felt bad was when my heart rate was elevated and my blood was really pumping.

He scheduled the stress test, and as soon as I finished, the nurse had me lie down. "Are you okay? Feeling dizzy?" I told her I felt okay, but I could tell from her expression and the way she hurried out of the room that she was worried. She came back a few seconds later with the doctor right behind her.

That's when I started to panic.

"Sir, we need you to stay calm," the nurse said.

The doctor looked at the test results and then back at me, clearly concerned.

"You telling me to 'stay calm' when y'all look so worried is *causing* me to freak out," I said. "What is going on? If you want me to 'stay calm,' you've gotta tell me what's happening!"

The doctor then explained that the test had confirmed my suspicion that something was wrong. My heart wasn't getting enough blood at those higher heart rates. When I was at rest, things were fine. But when I started working out, my heart couldn't keep up.

The doctor immediately scheduled a procedure to better understand what was going on and discovered that my left anterior descending (LAD) artery was 100 percent blocked. I learned later that the blocked LAD put me at risk for what doctors call a widow-maker heart attack. They call it that because so few people survive. More often than not, it's a one-and-done event that makes widows out of people.

With my LAD blocked, my heart compensated by growing from the good side to the blocked side to supply it with blood. That's why I felt fine when my heart rate and blood pressure were normal. It's also why, in the airport, my heart did what it did. It slowed me down to keep me from going into heart failure. The blockage explained why I felt chest pains and breathlessness when I was running or boxing. My heart was struggling to keep the blood flowing.

The doctor tried to put in a cardiac stent that same day, but the blockage was too severe. He scheduled me for open-heart surgery. A week before that procedure, my dad's best friend called and explained to me why I should try to avoid having my chest cracked open if at all possible. He worked at Baylor Hospital in Dallas, which has one of the best cardiology teams in the nation. Before I had the surgery, he wanted me to meet with a specialist at Baylor for a second opinion.

I agreed and took him the disk from the first unsuccessful stent procedure. After reviewing the video of the surgery, the Baylor cardiologist told me he was about 80 percent sure he could get a stent placed, which meant I could avoid major surgery. Eighty percent was good enough for me. On April 3, 2020, exactly one year and one day before the heart attack that almost took me out, the specialist put a stent in my heart to clear the path for blood flow. It worked, at least for a while.

The whole experience—from the heart attack at the airport to the stress test and the surgery—made me aware of the warning signs: chest pain, trouble breathing, feeling heavy and exhausted. Those warning signs helped save my life. Without them, I'd have never made it to the emergency clinic on time.

Could You Die Happy Today?

This isn't a book about near-death experiences. It's a book about living life to the fullest. My heart attack was a wake-up call, a powerful reminder that I have work to do. It took dying for me to realize the powerful calling on my life.

I am alive for a reason. You are too. I hope you realize that.

Flatlining that day also served as a warning not to waste a single moment.

If I had died—permanently—in that emergency clinic on Easter Sunday, it would have been with regrets. There is still a lot I want to do, things I could have done or achieved already if I hadn't wasted so many years of my life. Looking back on those "wasted" years now, though, I can count lesson after lesson that I learned, lessons that I'm grateful to carry into my future. In that sense, nothing is wasted.

Several years before my last heart attack, though, I habitually missed the lessons life was trying to teach me. During those years, despite the fact that I had money and what appeared to be a pretty great life, I felt lost and deeply dissatisfied.

Looks can be deceiving.

Can you relate? Maybe you've already accomplished so much, and you still know something is missing.

For years, I tried to fill that desire for more by chasing anything and everything that I thought would make me happy, from women to money to better clothes and nicer cars. When happiness eluded me, and depression closed in, I used drugs and alcohol to push away the feelings and fears I didn't want to face. It didn't work, and my life bordered on crashing. At the time, my code of behavior kept me trapped in a life I didn't want to live.

If your life is anything like mine was, the warnings signs are there. For me, it was toxic relationships with women, habits that made me feel terrible physically, mentally, and emotionally, friends who belittled my dreams, and a totally self-focused lifestyle. The thing is, I knew that none of those people or habits were good for me. I had seen and experienced a different—better—way of life. But even though I knew better, I kept drifting back to the things that ultimately made life *worse*.

Nashville was one of those places where it was easy for me to drift into old patterns. I worked at improving my health and mindset, but between friends and my girlfriend at the time, the temptation to party was always there. Life felt like a constant struggle between the kind of person I wanted to be and the people and habits that held me back.

9

I didn't want to admit it, but that girlfriend was someone who held me back. Don't get me wrong, she's a great person and has many solid qualities. A couple of instances, however, helped me realize that our lives and mindsets weren't in alignment. The first time I picked up on that came when we were discussing her plans for the future. She told me she wanted to be an event planner. My response was, "Badass! I love that idea!" With all the networking I did, I had already met some people in that space. My mental wheels started turning immediately. "How about you get goin' with a company so you can learn all the ins and outs of the business. When you've got a handle on it, I'll help you start a company."

She immediately shut down that idea. "Start my own company?" she asked. "I don't know. That would be a lot of work."

At that moment, a warning bell went off. *I am an entrepreneur*! Running your own company *is* a lot of work, but I really can't imagine my life any other way. To me, calling the shots and being free to build as big as I want, earn as much as I want, and with the people I want is worth every bit of time I put into building my businesses. The fact that she didn't get that was a clue, a warning sign, that we weren't a great fit.

Not long after that, we went to a local bar where she ordered a beer. She took a sip and said, "*Mmmmm*. God, I needed that." Those words set off another warning bell. Listen, there's nothing wrong with having a drink, but I had been working hard at not *needing* a drink. *Right then*, I knew I had to let her go. I knew there was no way I could expect to change my habits and really grow if I held on to that relationship because we were headed in two different directions.

Paying attention to the warning signs also helped me notice the habits and mindsets that worked *for* me rather than against me. I watched and learned from the examples of people I respected and wanted to be more like.

A few years into my new, more intentional way of life, that heart attack almost ended it all. I wasn't ready to go then. I *still* feel like I have so much left to do in this life. I'm glad God agreed and let me live. Every day that I wake up, I thank God for another day. Every night before I go to sleep, I thank him again. And in the hours in between, I show my gratitude for this gift of life by making the most of it.

What Are the Warning Signs in Your Life?

Chances are if your life isn't on track, you feel the tension between where you are and where you want to be. That tension is a warning sign that something isn't right. Here are a few common pains and discomforts that may indicate you need to make some changes in your life:

- Constantly comparing yourself to others
- Depression
- Broken relationships
- Loneliness
- Feelings of regret or shame
- Constant worry
- Feeling stuck
- An empty bank account
- Fear of the future
- Feelings of envy or inadequacy
- Lack of purpose

11

- Poor health
- A desire for more
- Feeling like something is missing
- Never satisfied

If any of the items on this list resonate with you, or if there are other symptoms you can add to the list, pay attention to the warning signs! Your life can be better, happier, and more fulfilling. Consider this book your crash cart. The defibrillator is charged up and ready to bring you back to life. Sometimes we all need a jolt of energy. Let this moment be your reawakening.

Are You Truly Living?

After bringing me back to life, the nurse and doctor worked with paramedics to load me in an ambulance and transfer me from the clinic to the hospital. Later, I learned many people who suffered the kind of heart attack I had die in the ambulance on the way to get treatment. I'm thankful God had other plans for me.

It turned out that the first stent wasn't fully in place and had gotten completely clogged. In emergency surgery, doctors put a second stent in the same spot as the first to clear the way for blood flow.

I awoke from that procedure with a renewed sense of gratitude. It sounds cliché, but, literally, the trees blooming outside the hospital window looked greener, and the spring sky seemed bluer.

Everything seemed more vibrant because I felt thankful to be alive. I was aware, too, that surviving meant I still had a purpose to fulfill. Three days later, I walked out wearing a hospital gown over my pants. (My shirt had been left back at the emergency clinic.)

Shockingly, my heart showed normal pumping function and no damage from the widow-maker event. That's what doctors call the kind of heart attack I experienced because so few people survive. The LAD funnels blood for the entire body. Typically, an LAD blockage cuts off blood flow and oxygen to the body and often ends up killing at least part of the heart. Somehow, miraculously, my heart survived without damage. That blessing isn't something I take lightly. I know I am still living for a reason, and part of that reason is to share this message with you:

You don't have to die to decide to live.

You don't have to die to decide to live.

I don't care how old you are, what your past looks like, what you have or haven't done, or what kind of traumas are in your past. You can make the decision right now to heed the warning signs and choose to live your life to the fullest. That's what this book is about: equipping you to be intentional with your thoughts and actions so you can experience *your* best life.

Other books might seek to achieve this same goal, but the path those books take to reaching this goal differs from this book.

I've discovered that until we change our code of behavior, nothing in our life changes. Thankfully, the flip side is true too. The moment we change our code of behavior is the moment we set our brand-new life in motion.

I don't believe in coincidence.

I believe in faith and hard work. I believe in rewards and consequences. I believe in the code of behavior: What you get out of life depends upon what you put into it.

My hope and prayer for this book is that what you read here will inspire you to stop living in fear, worry, negativity, and shame. I want your code of behavior to empower you to live with the kind of discipline that maximizes your abilities so you can achieve abundance and a fulfilling life. I want you to know you *can* go after your dreams and become the best version of yourself. You can live full out and, when the day comes, die without regrets.

Today is the day to truly start living.

Chapter 2
UNDERSTANDING THE CODE OF BEHAVIOR

We are what we repeatedly do.
Excellence, then, is not an act but a habit.

—Will Durant

WHEN I DIED on Easter Sunday of 2021 and walked out of the hospital three days later, I knew God had spared my life for a purpose bigger than I had ever imagined. You're part of that purpose.

Flatlining is pretty dramatic. There's no chance you can walk away from an experience like that without doing some reflection. That reflection planted the seed for this book.

Right before the heart attack, I was happy to be alive. My life was finally in a place where I felt good about who I was and how I showed up in other people's lives. But it hadn't always been that way. For many years, I struggled with drug and alcohol addiction, stayed stuck in unhealthy environments, relationships, and friendships, and just plain made bad choices. It took time, counseling, and transformation workshops to get to a place where I finally understood my purpose and the power of my true potential.

As I reflected on where I'd been, how far I'd come, and where I wanted to go with my new lease on life, the ideas in *The Code of Behavior* began to take shape. These ideas weren't new to me, in fact, I'd been living by different codes all my life.

The reality is you, too, are living by a code. It's your pattern of behavior, your habits, beliefs, mindsets—and the driving motivation behind them.

You probably don't call your habit of exercising every day—or not exercising at all—a code. The same goes for the way you think about money or relationships—or the way you neglect to think about those things. Whether you're doing something or not, you're living by a code of behavior. You may break from that code from time to time and do something out of the norm. If you're anything like the majority of humanity, however, your habits and mindsets will kick in and bring you back to the same patterns of behavior unless you intentionally change your code.

Changing your code is the key. You do that with discipline and over time. One of the biggest differences between successful people and unsuccessful people is that successful people do what is goal-achieving, not stress-relieving, until their goal-achieving habits become stress-relieving habits. We always fall back on our habits—our code of behavior.

When you fall back on the right habits and positive mindsets, you move a little closer toward your greatness every day. That's awesome.

If you fall back on habits and mindsets that keep you stuck in a life you don't want, that's *not* awesome. It's terrible. It's also where most people live—stuck, dissatisfied, and unhappy. That's why people walk around wearing shirts that say *Mondays Suck*. (I saw a college kid walking his dog the other day wearing a dinosaur mask and a shirt with *Mondays Suck* on it. I wanted to stop him and say, *If you change your mindset and what you do with it—change your code of behavior—then the way you feel about the day would be completely different. I love Mondays!*

(If I see him again, I'll give him a copy of this book.)

Here's the good news: Life doesn't have to suck on Monday or any other day of the week. You don't have to stay stuck. You can rewrite your personal code of behavior and start making your life awesome any time you want.

It's as simple as BC = LC.

Behavior Code = Life Change

The Code of Behavior Is Inescapable

Sow a thought, and you reap an act;
Sow an act, and you reap a habit;
Sow a habit, and you reap a character;
Sow a character, and you reap a destiny.

—Charles Reade

Humans have been following codes of behavior for thousands of years. One of the most well-known codes of behavior is the Ten Commandments. Even if you've never been to temple or church, you've probably heard of these ten rules for living. The Judeo-Christian world still follows this code to one degree or another. Literally etched into stone, the Ten Commandments

17

have withstood the test of time. Until the past few decades, it was common to find the Ten Commandments posted on, painted on, or carved into the walls of county courthouses across the United States.

This code is straightforward. It's good for the individual and society at large, addressing how to treat other people and love God. The Ten Commandments remind us to rest and not to kill, cheat, steal, lie, or compare ourselves to others. Fifteen hundred years after Moses delivered the Ten Commandments to the Jews, Jesus summarized this code into just two commands: Love God and love others. You can't find a much simpler code than that.

Religious codes like the Ten Commandments are only one example. You can find codes of behavior in almost every kind of group or organization.

- The United States Marine Corps is known for its code that is summed up by its motto *Semper Fidelis,* which emphasizes honor, courage, and commitment. The code of commitment is so deeply ingrained in the culture that you never refer to retired marines as ex-marines. Once a marine, always a marine.

- Schools—from preschools to universities—operate by defined codes of behavior. For little kids, the code is simple: Be kind, do your best, listen to the teacher and each other, and don't hit anyone. In college, professors define the code for the classroom. I remember one professor who had a rule that if you had four tardies or missed two classes, you were dropped. His code, or at least part of it, was you showed up on time every time class was in session. (By the way, I took issue with his code and dropped his class on the first day.

My code was more like, *if I can pass a class without having to be there, why bother?*)

- Businesses often post their core values and ethical standards in their facilities for their employees and guests to see. It's a way to hold everyone accountable to the established code of behavior. Everyone knows, for example, that Chick-fil-A is closed on Sundays. Taking Sunday off is part of the company's code to honor God, people, and the need for rest. That day off allows "operators and their team members to enjoy a day of rest, be with their families and loved ones, and worship if they choose."

- If you live in a neighborhood with a homeowner's association, you may get fined if you don't follow the code of behavior, which could include anything from how tall your grass can be to what color you paint your fence or to how late your July Fourth celebration can last.

- Clubs of all sorts operate by a code members must follow if they want to remain in good standing. "The first rule about fight club . . ." You might know the rest of that code even if you've never been *in* a fight club.

Not all codes of behavior are formalized. Think about the way you act around your family and friends. I'm betting the way you talk and act around your mother is different from the way you act around your closest friends. That's okay, and it's not being fake. I'm always myself, but part of connecting well with people is making them feel comfortable by knowing the code—even if it's unspoken. Think of it this way: You're going to wear different clothes to a business meeting than you would to the gym, but it's still *you* wearing the clothes.

You may have different codes for different friend groups. You might, for example, limit yourself to one or two drinks at happy hour when you're with friends from work. But when you're with your game-day buddies, you don't even think about limits. Or you may choose not to drink at all, depending on the company or your personal code.

No one sat you down and told you how to behave, except maybe your mom, who laid down the law when you were a kid and isn't about to let up now. (If you chew with your mouth open at dinner at my mom's house, you get invited to leave the table. It doesn't matter how old you are.) You developed your code by paying attention to people's responses to you, by gauging how comfortable or confident you felt in various situations, and by watching what the people around you said and did. Sometimes that works out okay, and sometimes it leads you down the road to destruction.

What Code Are You Living By?

Be the designer of your world and not merely the consumer of it.

—*James Clear,* Atomic Habits

Most people don't realize they're following a code of behavior. They just live their lives day after day, following along with the culture of their surroundings. That's normal. It's natural. If that's where you are right now, don't beat yourself up. Decide, instead, that today is the day to take control of the direction of your life.

I didn't understand I had a code of behavior until I was well into adulthood and started to intentionally spend time with people who were living differently from me. As the saying goes, birds of a feather flock together, and for years I had hung around people who, like me, enjoyed partying and taking life easy. In 2013, I started my journey of entrepreneurship and learned a completely different way to think, work, and live.

My first business mentor, Tim (whom my dad says is my guardian angel—well, one of them anyway), has a code of behavior that you get your ass up and get to work! No sleeping in or taking a bunch of naps. If you want a better life, you have to work for it. It took some getting used to because staying up all night had been the norm for me. But I wanted the life he had—or at least something like it—so I paid attention to what he was doing and worked every day to keep up. He taught me no one was going to save me. If I wanted something, I had to be willing to put in the work.

When I started to experience the results of following Tim's example, I finally understood how much control I had over my life. I also realized my behavior—positive or negative—produced rewards or consequences. That insight opened up a whole new world of possibilities for me. I always knew I wanted to do great things with my life, and I saw that with intention (or a goal) followed up by the right mindset and actions, I could accomplish anything.

Goal + Mindset + Disciplined Action = Results

My code had worked against me for years. I set the wrong goals (or failed to set any at all), operated from the wrong mindset (negative desires), and had either done the wrong things or not enough of the right things. As a result, I hadn't gotten very far in life.

When I set goals for what I wanted and who I wanted to become and then pursued them with a positive mindset and the right disciplined actions, my new code of behavior completely changed my life.

So what about you?

What is your current code of behavior?

How does that code affect your health, relationships, finances, or belief in your potential? Is it serving you well, moving you in the direction you want to go?

Are you drifting along? Are you completely stuck?

Everyone *wants* a great life, but few people are willing to put in the work to make it happen. If you're ready to make a change, you've got to get out of your own way. To be a champion, you have to do what champions do!

You might be wondering what champions do. In this book you're going to learn how to develop the code of a champion.

Excuses or Results

Nothing great was ever built on excuses.
You can't whine your way through life. Kick your inner
whiner's ass and get to living the good life.

—Bryant McGill

Change.

Some people thrive on change. Others dread it.

No matter which side of that love-hate relationship you fall on, change can be hard—which is why most people avoid change altogether.

Even when you know change is good for you and could lead to outcomes you actually want, maintaining the status quo feels easier. This leads to excuses, which lead to stagnation rather than results.

While I was waiting for a flight a while back, a guy walked up to me and said, "My wife and I are wondering what that 100/0 tattoo on your neck is about."

I have a bunch of tattoos, so I don't know what made them notice that one in particular, but the answer was easy: "It means take 100 percent responsibility for everywhere you are in life and everywhere you're not and make zero excuses," I told him.

He looked shocked. I don't know what answer he was expecting, but my guess is he didn't expect it to be a deep life philosophy. He took it in and then nodded and walked away. That's the response many people have to the idea of taking 100 percent responsibility for their lives.

Excuses are easy. Taking personal responsibility for where you are in life, well, that's another story. Unsuccessful people rely on excuses and make them part of their code. No one wants to admit it, but it's true. Do any of these sound familiar?

It's too hard to eat right when I'm traveling.

Yeah, I said some things I didn't mean, but she made me so mad.

I would have hit my goal last year if it hadn't been for the lockdown. I just don't have enough time.

Everyone was having fun, and I didn't want to miss out.

The government makes it impossible for my business to succeed. Taxes and inflation are just too high!

Do you have your own excuses to add to the list? Of course! We all do.

Excuses are a cop-out. The truth is, it rains on the rich just like it rains on the poor. Successful people have all the same reasons to make excuses.

Successful people travel.

They have to deal with difficult people.

They face challenges, like the global pandemic.

They have the same twenty-four hours in a day unsuccessful people have. They have to make hard choices.

They live in the same world with the same rules as everyone else.

The difference between unsuccessful people and people who experience success is that successful people don't make excuses. They make it happen. They are willing to do the work, go the extra mile, and find a solution.

No one gets out of this life without experiencing pain or difficulties or boredom or disappointment. Not long ago, someone took over one of my business locations. Part of the agreement was he would run the place and pay rent on the location. A few weeks in, the dude dipped—without paying—leaving me responsible for the rent. I could cover it, but that wasn't the point. He got bored or scared or whatever, and he made an excuse for not holding up to his end of the deal.

I was *heated*, but instead of wasting energy being mad or losing any more time or money on the deal, I focused on what I could control: finding someone who would take over and wouldn't make excuses. Within a few days, I found someone amazing, and he's rocking it.

You've got to focus on the solution because *everyone* has the opportunity to make excuses. Successful people push past the BS and acknowledge life could suck if they let it suck—or it could be great if *they* make it great. And then they do what it takes to live with excellence and reap the rewards.

Greatness is the intention of the successful person's code of behavior. Everything they do, think, say, and believe is part of that code. Making excuses doesn't fit into their code.

Excuses don't serve them.

Excuses or results, which will you choose? Remember: You can have excuses, or you can do what needs to be done.

My hope is you've picked up this book because you're ready to stop making excuses and start making a great life. You understand to get different outcomes, you must do life differently than you have in the past. I hope you realize, too, that you were born with the potential for greatness. We all are. Every person on the planet has unique talents and strengths just waiting to be explored and used. The sad thing is, relatively few people choose to tap into their true potential.

If you're ready to pursue your unique greatness, you may need a whole new code of behavior. At the very least, you're going to want to refine your current code—replacing some mindsets and habits with others that propel your success.

What's Your Code?

The life we experience is determined by our personal code of behavior. Up until now, you may not have called it a code. You were just living life, day after day, doing whatever it took to survive or keep up. But all that's about to change, starting now.

Now that you understand you're living by a code, you have the power to choose what you want that code to be. In the next few chapters, we're going to examine and implement the five essential elements to intentionally develop a code of behavior that pushes you toward greatness. Those five essentials are goals, desire, discipline, confidence, and action.

1. **Goals** give you something to aim for.

2. **Desire** gives you a reason not to give up.

3. **Discipline** empowers you to live by the code of behavior that yields the results you want.

4. **Confidence** gives you the mindset for success.

5. **Action** moves you from dreams to reality.

Without these five essentials, remember, you'll still have a code. It just won't get you where you want to go. In fact, without the essentials, you may not even know where you want to go.

At the end of each chapter, you will find a space for reflection called "What's Your Code?" I encourage you to take some time to consider what you've read and, most importantly, the code you're living by. The questions will guide you to examine four key aspects of your current code of behavior: your beliefs, attitudes, actions, and results. Use the space provided to make notes.

What do you **believe** about yourself and your future right now? Do you believe life has more to offer than what you're experiencing right now?

What or who do you want to **become**? Are you willing to make changes to your thoughts and habits to become your best self?

Does your current **behavior** support your goals and desires for your future? In other words, if you keep doing what you're doing, will you get where you want to go?

Based on the answer above, what kinds of behavior **belong** in your code? What behaviors do you already know you need to stop doing? What are a few behaviors you know you need to *start* doing?

Chapter 3
ESSENTIAL 1
GOALS

*When something is important enough, you do it even if
the odds are not in your favor.*

—Elon Musk

IN MAY OF 2013, I was living in the living room of a buddy's two-bedroom apartment alongside his friend in Santa Monica, California. I had sold all my stuff—except the clothes I'd taken with me in a trash bag—and had moved out there from Texas. My grandma and great-grandma couldn't stand the thought of me sleeping on the living room floor, so they bought me a bed because they knew I couldn't afford one. Space was tight and, with my bed in the living room, privacy was limited, but I didn't mind.

Like so many people, I'd gone to California to pursue a dream. I wanted to be an actor and a fitness model. Gigs were tough to find, but that was okay because I had started to build my first business. My life was busy and not at all luxurious, but for the first time in a long time, it felt like my life might actually be heading somewhere.

Before moving out to California, I was angry all the time—not just at other people. I was angry and frustrated with myself because I was so dissatisfied with my life. I had tried—hard—to go the conventional route: you know, go to college, earn a degree, go to work, and earn a paycheck.

The thing is, I had done all that, and it sucked. In an effort to get my life together, I went back to college at twenty-three and finished deeply in debt at twenty-seven. I mean thousands and thousands of dollars in debt. As a student, I had earned $4,000–$5,000 bartending at a club a few nights a week. When I graduated, I did the responsible thing and took a job in the real world selling digital media advertising space—a job that cut my income in half.

You read that right.

Instead of working twelve hours a week for $4,000–5,000 a month, I started working sixty hours a week for a whopping $2,000 a month.

Something didn't add up.

Besides being broke financially, I realized, after four years of classes and a few months at my corporate job, the "real world" wasn't where I wanted to be. I didn't want to be stuck in a cubicle for the rest of my life working for someone else's dream. If you have a corporate job you love, I'm happy for you, but I figured out pretty quickly it wasn't for me.

It wasn't just the paycheck or the cubicle I hated. The negativity of the environment drained me. Five days a week, I'd wedge myself into a packed elevator at 7:15 a.m. so I could be at my desk and on the phone by 7:30. Every morning, some company veteran would make the same joke: "Is it 4:30 yet?" I knew if the long-timers were still living paycheck to paycheck, watching the clock, and working for the weekend, that's what my future held if I stayed there. That wasn't the life I wanted.

A month before I moved to California, I ran into an old friend, Tim, at a nightclub. A friend and I had driven up to Oklahoma City, and somehow we all ended up in the same place. It was April 4, 2013. I remember the date because it was his birthday and he invited us back to his house for the after-party. I also remember the date because it was the beginning of a huge paradigm shift in my life.

We had met several years earlier through the party scene. He had worked as a trainer at a gym before he and a friend opened a private fitness studio together. Then the recession took him out, and he ended up losing everything. He was just getting started with a new business when I headed back to college to finish my degree at the University of North Texas.

Over the next four-and-a-half years, we caught up every once in a while when he would stop into the nightclub where I worked. He was excited about his business and would tell me all about how well he was doing and how much he was pulling in. Each time, I'd just serve him a drink and laugh it off.

Honestly, I thought he was one of those $30,000-a-year millionaires. I had met plenty of those while bartending.

It was hard to play it cool when we rolled up to his 10,000-square-foot house that night on his birthday. Sitting out front was a brand-new, totally decked-out Mercedes-Benz CLS 63 AMG. Next to it sat an L-series Autobiography Range Rover. Those cars cost more than $150,000 *each*.

We got to talking the next morning, and he told me what he was earning with his business. His *monthly* earnings were over four times higher than what I was earning a *year*. I was happy for him, and, at the same time, I felt like I'd been sucker punched. (Remember, I was taking home $2,000 a month after taxes from a job that had me stuck in a cubicle.) As much as I liked and respected Tim, I couldn't help but think, *Why him and not me? I mean, if he can do it, so could I, right?*

Tim invited me to attend a business seminar with him. I am so glad I agreed because it was there my life began to change. A couple of things I heard at the meeting shifted my perspective.

"We were not put on this earth to go to work, pay bills, and die."

"You can work to build your dreams, or somebody will hire you to build theirs."

The words resonated with me. *That's my life,* I realized. Right then and there, I decided to quit my corporate job.

I'm going to sell everything I have. I'm going to move to Los Angeles, and I'm chasing my dreams.

The company I worked for reaffirmed my decision the following Monday when the bosses refused to let the sales team go home until we hit $450,000 in sales for the day. At 4:30 p.m., we were at $425,000, and it took another half hour to hit $450,000. While I was stuck in traffic on the way home, the thought hit me, *Hold up! Those people are bringing in $450,000 a day, and I'm getting $2,000 a month? Hell naw!*

Now, I don't recommend doing this, but I took my vacation days, and never went back. Instead, headed to California. My dream of becoming an actor and fitness model was something I had always wanted to do. Sure, it was a risk. But I decided I would rather risk going after my dream, knowing if I didn't make it, at least I would have spent my life pursuing something I was passionate about instead of settling for doing something I hated for a paycheck.

What was cool about the whole thing was I had my mom and dad's support. My mom reminded me to focus on the potential to succeed when she said, "Look at how many people are successful, not how many aren't. If they can do it, I truly believe you can too."

My dad had a picture of me printed and wrote a long note on the back telling me to "go kick some major ass out there!"

With their support and my own belief, I figured, If I am going to take a risk on something, it might as well be myself because I'm the only thing in this world I can control.

During the previous four-and-a-half years, Tim had occasionally reached out to me to talk about what he was doing to change his life and his bank account. It wasn't until I was pissed at living paycheck to paycheck, working on someone else's dream instead of my own, that I really listened. Armed with new inspiration, I started a side hustle of my own with a health and wellness business. Entrepreneurship hadn't been on my radar, but after learning what was possible, I committed to building a business on the side while I pursued my dream of fitness modeling and acting.

Bartending was my backup plan for money, but it turned out I didn't need it. In my first month of working for myself, I earned $1,900—for way fewer hours than I had in my corporate job. I didn't really even know what I was doing other than following Tim's advice on the business. It was easy to see the potential of what could happen if I focused on my side hustle. I shifted my focus to building my business, and I loved it. I felt great, and I enjoyed helping other people feel better about their health and wellness. I was also building a team of business partners who were excited about helping other people live fit.

Tim stayed in touch, mentoring me from halfway across the country. Five weeks later, he invited me to come and stay with him for a while at his home in Oklahoma 1) so I could see what his life was really like, and 2) so I could learn from him. I agreed, and that decision changed everything for me.

What are you willing to give up to go up? I had only been in California for five weeks. I had dreamed of living there my entire life, and I loved it. When Tim made that offer, though, I knew I had to go. In a short time, I had gotten a glimpse of my business's potential. I knew that if I focused my time and energy and had someone who really believed in me coaching me on how to succeed, there was no limit to what I could do. Moving was an easy decision for me because I had a vision for what was possible and wanted to go for it.

Today I pay more in taxes annually than what I earned per year in my corporate job. I regularly get invited to speak to audiences around the world about what I did to change my life so dramatically in such a short time. These days, the topic always comes back to the heart attack. I don't mind that, honestly. If talking about dying helps people realize *now* is the time to take control of their lives and go after their dreams, I'm happy to tell that part of my story, even if it makes me cry every damn time. But what I really want to share with them—what I want to share with you in this book—is how our choices shape our lives. Our choices shape our code of behavior and determine the kind of lives we live.

Actor Jim Carrey said, "You can fail at what you don't want, so you might as well take a chance on doing what you love." That's what I decided to do back in 2013. I drew a line in the concrete because I was tired of living the way I was. That choice has made all the difference in my life. Understand this: It's our

> It's our choices—not our circumstances, not our childhood traumas, not even a global pandemic—that make or break us.

choices—not our circumstances, not our childhood traumas, not even a global pandemic—that make or break us.

It was the choice I made to take a chance on myself, to listen to and learn from a mentor, to stop making excuses and start doing the necessary work, day in and day out—and eventually, to define my own code of behavior—that enabled me to become the person I am today. Let me tell you: I had a long way to travel from the person I was in my teens and twenties to the person I am now at thirty-six. Guess what? I still have a long way to go to become the person I want to be. I'm still making choices that stretch me every day mentally and physically.

So how do I know what choices to make? How can *you* make better choices for your life?

How can you know which choices will move you in the right direction?

First things first, you have to know the direction you want to go. In other words, you have to set a goal.

What Do YOU Want?

Most people fail in life not because they aim too high and miss, but because they aim too low and hit.

—Les Brown

When I made the choice to pursue entrepreneurship, my immediate goal was to build a business that would actually pay my bills. My bigger dream, though, was to live like Tim was living. I quickly achieved my first goal, which put me on the path for the life and lifestyle I wanted. Then I set a new goal and achieved it. Set, achieve, repeat. Today I have *massive* goals.

Goals give you a target—something to shoot for. Without a goal, you don't know where to aim or what actions to take, which means you can end up working your ass off and not getting anywhere. That's not how I wanted to live, and it's not what I want for you either. That's why having a goal is the first of the five essentials to developing your code of behavior. When you align your goals with a code of behavior that pushes you to achieve, you will move closer to the life you want every day.

You have to know what you want, so you know what choices are right for you. If you want to become a world-class athlete, your daily activities will be different from those of a person who wants to build a multimillion-dollar business, but your code—the principles you live by—will be the same. It's a code of self-discipline and a killer work ethic. To become the best at whatever you do, your code must be one of excellence, regardless of the specific activities you do day-to-day to fulfill your goal's unique requirements.

When my mentor invited me to move from California to Oklahoma City to learn from him day in and day out, I immediately said yes. (I would have been a fool to say no to that!) In the short time I'd been working with him, I had already learned a ton—things no one ever taught in business school—about mindset and discipline. What I learned made me take a hard look at my lifestyle and limited success and see greater possibilities for myself.

With my desire reawakened, I packed up my trash bag and moved from California to Oklahoma City to see what else I could learn. I wanted Tim's lifestyle, which meant I needed to learn from him and do what he was doing. (I also had to stop listening to the friends who were telling me I would never succeed). Even back then, I understood I shouldn't take advice from people with whom I wouldn't trade places.

By this time in his career, Tim was a millionaire, as were many of his friends—except me, of course. I was a bartending, aspiring modeling, newbie entrepreneur. Although a bit clueless at the time, I was hungry for more, and I was no longer afraid to let it show.

After being around the kind of energy that poured off Tim and his friends and hearing their philosophies about business and life, I tapped into a bigger vision for myself. Even as I made plans for my future life, though, mindsets and bills from my past (I'm looking at you, student loans and credit cards) kept me anchored in the present. I was living and hanging out on a regular basis with millionaires, but I still kept a close eye on my budget. By that time, I was earning a decent living from my business, far more than I had when I worked for corporate or even when I was bartending, but I was still very aware of the costs of daily life and the bills I had to pay.

One day, Tim and I were driving through town on our way to a meeting when I commented on how much lower the gas prices in Oklahoma were compared to California.

"Really?" Tim asked. "I hadn't noticed. Come to think of it, I haven't paid attention to the price of gas in years."

Why would he? He was driving us around in a jacked-up F-250 that, with all the add-ons, was worth more than $100,000. A few bucks higher or lower at the pump wouldn't have made a difference to him the way they did to me. He didn't have to watch every penny like I did.

Then he said something that changed the way I thought about my money goals forever: "Why don't you stop focusing on budgeting and cutting things out and start focusing on making more money? Go help more people. Contribute to others' lives. Focus on growth and abundance rather than retreating."

Damn. If he weren't driving and had been holding a mic, he could have dropped it and walked away.

From that point on, my mindset about my financial goals shifted. Sure, to this day, I still set money-related goals, but the reason for setting a nine-figure target isn't just so I can buy a new car or even a jet. The purpose behind my financial goals today has to do with what Tim said that day in the truck about focusing on abundance and helping people. The money I earn is a representation of the lives I've been able to impact. With a deeper purpose in mind (something we'll look at more in the next chapter), my goals felt more important than ever.

What Does a Worthy Goal Look Like?

Goals are pure fantasy unless you have a specific plan to achieve them.

—Stephen Covey

Living without meaningful goals can feel like stepping on your car's gas pedal with one foot and smashing the brake with the other. You might make a whole bunch of noise but no forward progress. Do it too often or for too long, and it will damage your engine and ruin the tread on your tires.

Unfocused effort is exhausting and ineffective.

A worthy, code-defining goal is personal. Setting a goal to do something just because someone else is doing it isn't going to keep you inspired—neither will setting a goal because you think it will make someone else happy. Tons of kids go to college to make their parents happy. There are countless dissatisfied doctors and lawyers in this world who joined those ranks to please their parents. Now they're slogging through their days, well-paid but miserable. The point: You can have a fat bank account and still be unfulfilled.

Take a few minutes right now to visualize what you want most right now for your life, your relationships, your business or career, your financial status, your health and well-being. Can you picture what you will feel like when you achieve those goals?

I'm going to be honest with you—there was a time when I couldn't.

Early on in my career as an entrepreneur, I would say my goal was to make it to the top 1 percent in sales in the company I work with. I'd set the goal, but my work ethic and effort didn't match what I said I wanted.

One day, I attended a seminar where the speaker asked us to close our eyes and imagine what it would look like when we reached our goals and were recognized for our achievements. She told us to visualize what we would be wearing, what music would play as we took the stage, and who would be there to celebrate with us.

When I closed my eyes, I saw black. *Nothing!* My dreams were dead. I literally couldn't visualize achieving my goal because I was living by the wrong code. I wasn't showing up how I needed to show up, and I wasn't being the kind of person I needed to be to make it to the level of success I wanted.

The blackness scared me at first. It was a little like being back on that emergency clinic's table when the whole world went black. The exercise showed me that my code of behavior and lack of intentionality and effort were blocking me from seeing the future I wanted.

To make my goals a reality, I had to be honest with myself about how I was showing up. I had to adjust my code of behavior to match the level of success I wanted to achieve in my business.

As you think about the goal(s), visualize yourself achieving your milestone *and* your massive goals. If the future is hazy, check your code of behavior. Decide to become the person who is willing to put in the work and win big.

Then, as you identify your goals for the month, year, or even the next decade, make them personal and SMART. Here are a few things to keep in mind:

Your goal doesn't have to make sense to anyone but you. You must want your goal so badly you're willing to work for it day after day until you make it a reality.

Your goal must be personal. You can't control anyone else. Setting a goal to make someone happy may sound noble, but it isn't going to work. Happiness is a choice. You can't make someone else happy long term. It's an inside job. People have to be happy with *themselves*. Rather than trying to please others with your goals, focus on what *you* can do, have, and become. Others will benefit only when you're living at your best.

Your goal must be SMART. You've probably heard the acronym. Specific. Measurable. Attainable. Relevant/Realistic. Time-bound. Those five elements are like the rings on a target. They focus your attention and your effort so you don't waste time spinning your wheels. Let's break them down, one at a time.

Specific—What exactly do you want to achieve? Be as specific as you can when you set a goal.

- Setting a goal to "earn more" is far less meaningful than setting a goal to pay off an exact amount of debt or to earn enough to buy season tickets for your favorite team's events.

- Rather than saying I want to lose weight, put a number on your goal (e.g., "My goal is to lose _____ pounds," or "My goal weight is _____," or "I want to drop _____ pant sizes.").

- What is the exact figure you'll need to hit to reach your sales, customer retention, or profit goals?

Measurable—Making your goal measurable allows you to plan and track your progress. Most specific goals are measurable by default. But what if your goal is being a great spouse or partner? How are you going to measure that? One way is to define what *great* means. It might mean asking about the other person's day and really listening to their answer. It might mean setting aside time to spend together each day or every week. Those are actions you can track.

Attainable—When you think about what you want to achieve, ask yourself whether the goal is feasible given enough work and dedication. Pay attention here, though: *Attainable doesn't mean easy.* I want you to dream *big.* Your goal may seem impossible when you set it. If you want to experience extraordinary success, you have to set goals that shove you out of your comfort zone and make you reach higher and work harder than ever before.

You may have no idea at the moment how you will achieve the goal. That's okay. Sometimes the only way to discover how to reach a goal is to make your intentions clear. Don't get hung up on the fact that you don't know how to reach your goal yet. Ask: *Do I have, or can I acquire, the resources, knowledge, and skills to achieve my goal?* If your answer is yes, then set the goal and start striving. Every small success you have will push you toward your larger goal. The *how* becomes evident when you put your focus on what you want. With enough of the small successes, what once seemed impossible will become "I'm possible," and you will nail even the biggest goals.

Relevant/Realistic—Does the goal make sense in the larger scope of your life? Would achieving it move you closer to being the kind of person you want to become? A goal doesn't have to be a lifelong commitment. I set a goal to be a fitness model. It wasn't necessarily the career I wanted forever, but it was important to me to pursue—even for a short time. That act of courage and believing I was worth the risk set off a chain of events that changed my life.

Personally, I like going for goals that seem completely unrealistic to others. (Remember: Your goal only has to make sense to you.) Right now, one of my goals is to purchase a plane. Some people just don't get that kind of goal. They laugh at me or tell me I'm crazy to want something like that. You know what? Their response fires me up and makes me work even harder! I love proving the naysayers wrong.

Time-bound—Someday isn't a day of the week. In fact, *someday* is code for never. When I decided to write a book, I set the launch date for April 4, 2022—one year from the day I died. That date is personal to me. It's the day I got a second chance at life, and for me, that date was non- negotiable. Choose a deadline for each of your goals. Put the date on the calendar and schedule the celebration as an incentive.

Write down your goals and review them regularly. Nothing happens without focus and a plan of action. Writing down your personally meaningful SMART goal helps ingrain your intention in your psyche. One recent study shows you increase your odds of achieving your goal by more than 42 percent simply by recording it in writing. Grant Cardone, author of *The 10X Rule*, writes his goals down every morning and every night. "I want to wake up to it. I want to go to sleep to it, and I want to dream with it . . . I want to write my goals down before I go to sleep at night because they are important to me, they are valuable to me, and I get to wake up to them again tomorrow," he explains.

Create a plan of action. Knowing what you want is only part of the equation. A goal without an action plan is only a wish. Imagining what your life could look like is fun, but faith without action is dead. When you fail to follow up on your dreams with action, you'll end up feeling discouraged and depressed.

What do you need to do to achieve your goals? Whatever your goal is, identify the steps you'll need to take each day to achieve them by your deadline. Be specific.

- If your goal is to pay off your credit cards by the end of the year, figure out how much you need to put toward them each month (factoring in interest) to make that happen. How much will you have to earn each week and each day to make enough extra income to reach that goal?

- If you want to lose three pant sizes, how are you going to fuel your body and burn the necessary calories? What do you need to cut out of your diet? When and how are you going to get your exercise in? I'm a wellness coach, so I am always working on a health goal. Fitness and well-being are super important to me because I know that when people feel healthy and strong, they can achieve more in every area of life.

Learn more about Jason's Fitness Coaching Program

- If you have a profit goal, how *specifically* are you going to achieve it? Do you need to sell a certain number of products or programs? How many new clients do you need to acquire to make that happen? How many potential clients do you need to speak to each day to close that number of sales?

Your code of behavior ties into your goals and your plan of action. When you know what you want and have outlined the steps to achieving it, you're setting the standards for your code of behavior.

Play Full Out

*Every life-form seems to strive to its maximum
except human beings. How tall will a tree grow?
As tall as it possibly can. Human beings, on the other hand,
have been given the dignity of choice. You can choose to be
all, or you can choose to be less. Why not stretch up to the full
measure of the challenge and see what all you can do?*

—Jim Rohn

When you're setting a goal that will establish the framework for your code of behavior, it has to be significant—something worthy of your time, energy, and focus. There's no point in playing small! Think about it this way: If you were going to play the lottery, would you play to win $1 million—or $100 million? No one is going to give up $1 million, but if $100 million takes the same effort, why not go for the grand prize?!

Set the bar high. Dream *big*! As the quote from Jim Rohn notes above, you have the "dignity of choice." You can play full out to your maximum potential, or you can decide to coast along in an average life. Which life are you going to choose?

Grant Cardone's book *The 10X Rule* is one of my favorites on the topic of achieving huge goals. In it, he encourages readers to "dream at levels previously unimaginable." *Unimaginable*. This goes back to what I said earlier about setting impossible goals that may even seem unrealistic to others. Go after *crazy*, audacious goals. Whatever goal first comes to mind, double it. Better yet, multiply it by ten. Don't let your current situation limit your thinking. Dream *big*. If you're tired, you're not inspired—your goal isn't exciting enough. Dream even bigger!

Big goals inspire me. I have big goals, and I have big reasons for achieving them, but my goals have changed over time. When I first started out, my goals were about me—what I needed and wanted. The more I've achieved and matured, the clearer it has become to me that to be truly happy, to play at my optimal level, and to "stretch to up to the full measure of the challenge," my goals can't be all about me.

The same is true for you, which is why we're going to talk about understanding the power of purpose and the driving motivation behind your goals in the second essential of your code of behavior: *desire*.

Before you move on, take some time to dream big. What do you want to achieve? Check your goal against the requirements for a worthy goal, and then create a plan of action.

What's Your Code?

List the goals you have for your life right now.

1 Month Goal(s)

6 Month Goal(s)

1 Year Goal(s)

3 Year Goal(s)

5 Year Goal(s)

What do you **believe** about your ability to achieve your goals? Do you think they are too big? Not big enough? If you were going to 10X your goal, what would that look like?

What would it take for you to **become** the person who can achieve the goals you've set for yourself? Visualize yourself having accomplished your biggest goal. What does your life look like in that mental picture?

Does your current **behavior** support your beliefs and desires for your future? In other words, will your current behavior enable you to reach your goals?

With your goals in mind, what behaviors **belong** in your code? What do you need to start doing or do more of to achieve your goals? What do you need to stop doing?

Chapter 4
ESSENTIAL 2
DESIRE

There is one quality which one must possess to win, and that is definiteness of purpose, the knowledge of what one wants, and a burning desire to possess it.

—Napoleon Hill

MOST OF THE time, we don't consciously think, *I'm just going to follow the crowd,* or *I'm doing this because everyone else is doing it.* We just do it.

At least that was true for me when I started drinking at sixteen. A friend handed me a beer, and I took it. It didn't matter that I knew it was against the law or that my mom would be mad if she found out. My friends were drinking, and I didn't want to be laughed at for saying no. I also didn't want to miss out on a good time, which is what I thought drinking led to. So I took my first sip. And then another. And another. The more I drank, the more I felt like I fit in.

The same thing happened the first time someone handed me a joint. Everyone else was smoking, so I did too.

Then at seventeen, I tried cocaine for the first time because everyone else was using it. *Wow.*

That kind of high was like nothing I'd ever felt before, and I wanted more.

My friends call me an extremist. They're not wrong: When I'm into something, I'm all in, 100 percent. That trait has worked for me in many positive ways. It has helped me reach huge goals and become a high-income earner. When it came to alcohol and drugs, though, my extremist personality very nearly killed me. I wouldn't stop until the bottle was empty or the drugs were gone.

What started with drinking when I was a teen so I could fit in spiraled—and kept spiraling for years. It's a miracle I made it to adulthood and eventually into a very successful career. I would cut back for a while, but when I partied, I partied hard. And I *loved* to party—the nightlife, the drinking. I even loved the drugs. I loved being in the moment, feeling good—or not feeling at all. I loved being surrounded by beautiful women who liked to party as long and as wild as me.

But it was such an empty life.

I would go for hours and then wouldn't be able to sleep because of all the chemicals running through my system. Coming down from the high felt *horrible*. For the next few days, I was basically useless. It's hard to work when you can't think straight and the room is spinning. When my mind would clear, I'd realize how little I'd gotten done, which made me feel like crap. To feel better, guess what? I'd start drinking and working on getting high again to take the edge off the self-loathing. It didn't take long to fall into a routine—a trap—of using more often than not because that was what kept me feeling good.

Little by little, I recognized the tension between who I was and who I wanted to be. Some of that recognition came from maturity. Much of it came from spending time with people who were more successful than me.

I watched what my mentors were doing and noticed what they *weren't* doing. They weren't partying all night. Several of them were in committed relationships. All of their bank accounts far exceeded my own. They were intentionally making a difference with their lives rather than wasting their days recovering from partying too hard. The more I paid attention to the tension—the differences between the people I admired and how my own life was going—the clearer it became that if I wanted my life to change, it was up to me to change it.

Change, however, is rarely easy, and habits can be hard to break—especially when you're surrounded by people who have the same bad habits as you. Birds of a feather flock—or in my case, party—together.

Time after time, I would wake up the morning after a party and think, *I know better. Why do I keep doing this?* Right then and there, I'd say, "That's it! I'm done. No more!"

Willpower and guilt worked—for a while. I'd stay sober for a few weeks, maybe even a few months, but any time self-doubt surfaced, a relationship ended, or I had a really bad week, I'd give in to the desire to feel good "just one more time." Can you relate?

If you've been saying, "Just one more time," and then waking up with regret, it's time to stop fooling yourself. Your "one more time" lie doesn't have to be related to using drugs or excessive alcohol like a bandage to cover up your pain so that you don't have to deal with it.

It might be about any number of habits that you know you need to break:

- Indulging in an unhealthy relationship.

- Using a credit card when you know you don't have the money to pay off a big purchase.

- Hitting the snooze button and skipping a workout or going back for a second helping of dessert.

- Scrolling through social media or watching another YouTube or TikTok video when what you really need to do is put down the phone and get to work on yourself.

What's your vice?

What's the thing or person or habit you keep going back to "one more time"?

Listen: You can say, "Just one more time," every single day for the rest of your life and never break free from whatever or whoever is holding you back from becoming the best version of yourself. Some people do.

Giving in to the desire to fit in and avoid rejection or feel comfortable, loved, happy, or a little less fearful is natural. Saying yes to the things we desire is easy, and besides that, saying yes feels good! Every time you give in to your desires, you get a hit of dopamine, which reinforces the very behavior you want to stop or change. Eventually, however, that good feeling wears off, so you fall into a cycle of "one more time."

Desire is that powerful. And when you combine unhealthy desires, like wanting to fit in or feel numb to pain, with the wrong environment (and the wrong people), you have a recipe for disaster. When you flip things around and spend time with the right people and focus on what it takes to become the best version of yourself, your desires start to change.

Success is predictable. Don't overcomplicate it. The code is simple and consistent. When you do the right things, success is within reach.

Are You Driven by Fear or Faith?

Never let your fear decide your fate.

—Aaron Bruno

Do you remember the cartoons where a little angel popped up on one shoulder and a tiny devil appeared on the other when the main character was faced with a choice? That's the visual of desire. It comes in two forms: negative and positive. What you want and what you don't want. What you're desperate to achieve or have or become and what you dread. The prize and the punishment.

The temporary feel-good hit we get when we give in to self-gratification keeps us coming back for more. That feeling can seem almost impossible to resist, even if we know it's a fleeting prize. But there's something even stronger that keeps us locked in unproductive and unhealthy behavior patterns: fear.

Fear—avoiding what we don't want—is the force that drives most people to action or keeps them stuck even when they're miserable. See if any of these scenarios sound familiar:

- You fear the unknown, so you don't let yourself go there.

- You fear what people will think about you if you fail (or succeed), so you don't try.

- You fear being alone, so you stay in a toxic relationship.

- You fear getting dumped, so you stay single.

- You don't tell people about your dreams or what goals you've set for yourself because you don't want to give people ammo for holding you accountable or laughing at you if you screw up.

- You aren't sure you have what it takes to succeed in a new career, a new business opportunity, or a new relationship, so rather than risk it, you maintain the status quo.

How do I know?

Because that's where I was mentally when I was trying to follow along with what everyone else was doing. It's also where so many of the people I talk to every day are living. They are dissatisfied, broke, or stressed out because they fear the unknown that stands between them and where they want to be.

Fear wraps around us like darkness. It makes it hard to see beyond right now, so we start believing right now is all there is. We accept whatever life hands us, and then we work to maintain what is rather than focus on what *could be*.

If that's where you are, guess what? You're normal. You're experiencing the natural human state. Negativity is natural. Humans have a negativity bias. Our brains are wired for survival and will do whatever it takes to protect us. Call it whatever you want: fear, doubt, cynicism, realism, caution. Our natural negativity bias is what keeps us safe—and stuck.

We can be our greatest asset or our biggest liability. You've got to get out of your own way!

When I decided to get unstuck and design my life, I was beyond scared. Entrepreneurship is a scary path! (Anyone who tells you differently is lying.) Stepping out in faith into the realm of the unknown and away from a guaranteed paycheck is terrifying. But let's get real: Living paycheck to paycheck is a scary thing as well.

Fear Only Wins If You Let It

Do the thing you fear to do and keep on doing it . . .
that is the quickest and surest way ever
yet discovered to conquer fear.

—Dale Carnegie

Our greatness lies on the other side of fear. If we can get past our fears, we can usually look back and wonder what we were ever afraid of in the first place.

That's what happened to me when I went skydiving.

I thought about skydiving for fifteen years. I so badly wanted to do it, and, at the same, well, I was scared. Finally, I told myself, *Once I hit the top 1 percent, I'm gonna do it.*

The month after I hit my goal, I took a business incentive trip to Hawaii and put skydiving on the itinerary. To lock myself in, I invited friends to skydive with me.

A solid squad joined me that day, and it was a good thing they were there. I was so nervous that I tried to back out at the last minute, but my friends and my pride wouldn't let me.

We climbed into a tiny plane and headed up into the sky with the door open. Watching the world getting smaller below, I thought, *WTF am I doing?*

I thought the same thing again when the first people dropped from the plane and instantly became dots in the sky.

When I was next in line, I hyped myself up: *HERE WE GO, BABY!*

Three, two, ONE—and we jumped.

Flying—freefalling—was hands down the best experience of my life. I didn't want it to end. It was a *blast*! My only regret was that I should have jumped at fourteen thousand feet rather than twelve thousand. (Next time.)

By the time I landed, I'd forgotten why I was ever scared in the first place.

Fear too often stops us from doing what we want. We are conditioned to respond to fear by taking the safe and predictable path. But it's when we step off that path that the real fun begins.

When I stepped into entrepreneurship, so many people tried to push me back into the corporate world. Isn't it interesting, when you go to college, people cheer you on? They applaud when you take a risk and borrow tens of thousands or even hundreds of thousands in student loans for a career you aren't even sure you'll enjoy. Then they congratulate you when you accept a corporate position earning an annual salary that's a tiny percentage of what you owe.

If you tell those same folks you're going into business for yourself—you have a plan for earning more per year than a corporate job could ever offer—they will use fearful warnings to pull you back to the *real world*:

"Hold up. Working for yourself is risky." "You have no guarantees you'll succeed." "What about health insurance and your 401K?"

When I stepped into entrepreneurship, people shared their negativity bias in a cacophony of criticism. People told me the business model would never work. Some told me I was dumb for giving up my steady paycheck. Others said I would never succeed in the health and wellness industry because there was too much competition out there already. A few people literally laughed in my face.

I'm so glad I didn't listen to those people.

I'm going to pause here to acknowledge you may be wondering what I do since I haven't mentioned my specific business. That's on purpose because it doesn't matter. The code of behavior we're focusing on developing in your life isn't dependent on a particular business model or industry.

I am convinced you can apply the five essentials of goals, desire, discipline, confidence, and action to *any* business, relationship, or life plan—and *win*. It's who you become in the process of defining and then living out these essentials that gets you closer to being the best version of yourself.

> You can apply the five essentials of goals, desire, discipline, confidence, and action to *any* business, relationship, or life plan— and *win*.

I know for a fact that when you change your code of behavior to achieve your goal, whatever it is, there will be people who throw the same kind of negative noise at you. I call the people who toss out doubts like grenades aimed at blowing up others' ambitions *dream killers*. They operate from a place of fear. They think it's their responsibility to bring you back to your senses any time you set out to try something new or out of the norm. Don't follow them back to the darkness of fear and let their opinions become your reality! If you let them win, they will ruin your vision for the future.

Whenever a dream killer says, "You'll never succeed," I have to remember that statement is a direct reflection of how they feel about themselves. That's *their* fear talking. It has nothing to do with me.

My response to fear was to commit 100 percent to my goal. I had a clear path lined out by my mentors. I knew what to do, and I knew what I had to stop doing if I was really going to change my life. I decided to go all in and give my dream everything I had until it became a reality.

If you want to beat fear, you can't just try. Trying is the cousin of failure. You can't just say you'll "give it a shot and see how it goes." You've got to *commit*. You have to say, "This is what I'm doing, no matter what!" And then you have to *do it*, realizing if you're going to take a risk on anything, it might as well be yourself because you're the only thing you can control.

Will it be scary? No doubt.

> If you're going to take a risk on anything, it might as well be yourself because you're the only thing you can control.

Is there a chance you will fail before you succeed? A 100 percent chance!

But fighting through fear and living the life of your dreams is worth the risk, and I must say, proving the dream killers wrong is pretty nice, too. That's how you get to where *you* want to go. That's how you discover the greatness within yourself and become the person you were meant to be. You—your goals and dreams—are worth the risk.

Develop a Code of Behavior Founded on Faith

Successful people have fear, successful people have doubts,
and successful people have worries.
They just don't let these feelings stop them.

—T. Harv Eker

You have a choice: You can let fear control you, or you can choose to operate in the faith that you have options, unlimited potential, and the power to transform your life.

I decided long ago to make faith my MO (*modus operandi*). To protect myself from those dream killers and their doubt grenades, I had to do more than figure out what I wanted to do (my goal). I had to figure out *why* I wanted to accomplish it, I had to shift my focus (my desire) to what I wanted instead of what I feared, and I had to create the kind of environment that would push me toward my goal and my greater purpose.

The same is true for you.

In the next few pages, we'll focus on creating a code of behavior that makes faith, rather than fear, your driving motivation and power source. I'm not talking here about faith in terms of spirituality necessarily, although my spiritual faith is essential to who I am. I'm talking about faith in terms of belief in yourself and the potential you have for greatness.

Define Your Why

When your why is big enough, you will find your how.

—Les Brown

It's great to have a goal, but if you're going to find the strength to stick with your goal even when things seem to be falling apart, you have to know *why* you want it.

Knowing your why—the real reason for your goal—makes all the difference when it comes to fighting off fear and pushing ahead when flying shrapnel makes you want to hide instead of hustle. Your why feeds your faith and gives you a purpose beyond the prize.

What is the real reason for the goal you stated in the last chapter? What is your why?

Most people set goals without thinking about their whys. That's why it's easy for them to give up. They pick a target that sounds good, but they don't stop to understand why it appeals to them.

You might have set a financial goal, for example, to earn an additional $50,000 in the next twelve months. But why? What will extra income do for you? Do you want to buy a new house, pay for a child's college tuition, pay off debt, pay for a loved one's medical expenses? If money is your goal, how will you use it?

Once you have identified how you'll use that money, ask why again. Why is it important for you to pay off debt or buy a new house?

More money is not the real goal. The why behind it is the goal. That's true for any goal. If your goal is to get into better physical shape, ask why.

If your goal is to build a bigger business, ask why.

If your goal is to meet a life partner or deepen an existing relationship, ask why. If your goal is to learn a new skill, ask why.

Then ask why that reason is important to you. If you ask why long enough—and answer honestly—you'll find the why that touches your soul.

I've gone through this exercise with so many people, and they often get emotional when they get down to the core reason for wanting to achieve their stated goal. That *why* is the one that brings tears to their eyes and pushes them to keep going.

Without a strong enough why, you'll quit when things get tough. And things are going to get tough on the path to success. I've had so many reasons to quit in the past few years.

On December 26, 2019, I lost my little brother to drug addiction.

On April 3, 2020, I had heart surgery. Later that year, a family member took her life. On April 4, 2021, my heart stopped.

But the thing is, I'm still here because my why is stronger than the desire to give up.

I keep setting new and bigger goals for myself because my life, my *why*, is not about me! My why—my purpose for striving harder and constantly trying to get better—is about my mother, my grandmother, my father, my girlfriend, and my family to come. It's about all the people out there who need someone to believe in them. It's about helping others discover their true potential and transform their lives. That's what keeps me going. Every time I see someone I've worked with achieve *their* goals, my faith in my purpose grows. My *why* feeds my faith and my desire to keep going.

My challenge for you is to do the work to figure out why you want to achieve your goal.

Keep asking why until you get to the core motivator for your goal.

Shift Your Desire

> *Feed your faith and starve your doubts.*
> **—John C. Maxwell**

I wrote earlier about the power of desire and how it can work for you or against you. On the negative side, fear and doubt can paralyze you. When your focus is on avoiding what you don't want—be it pain, failure, disappointment, or rejection—the desire for relief in the form of a dopamine hit or others' acceptance can keep you stuck in destructive, dissatisfying patterns. It's like being imprisoned in your own mind.

On the positive side, you hold the key to escaping that prison. When you choose to shift your focus and energy to desires that feed your faith—like your *why*—you can transform your life!

When you shift your desire to align with your goals and what you want for your life, you'll get that same hit of dopamine every time you experience a win. Each step you make in faith expands your vision for what's possible—and it feels good!

Shifting your focus, however, isn't easy. What's easy is focusing on the negative. The trouble is what you focus on always grows. If you're focused on what you don't want—pain, disappointment, or rejection—odds are, that's exactly what you'll get. You bring about what you think about. If all you do is think about disappointment or negativity, that's what keeps showing up.

This reality shows up in all kinds of ways in our lives—from the simple to the life changing—and there's a neurological reason for it. The reticular activating system (RAS) connects the subconscious brain with the conscious brain. Its job is to filter out what you don't need to pay attention to, while at the same time, bringing what you *do* need to focus on to your conscious attention. By choosing to focus on what you want, you activate the RAS so that it notices more of what you want—more opportunities, more happiness, more things to be grateful for.

One simple example is the phenomenon that happens when you buy a new car. Suddenly you see other people driving that same car everywhere. Before you bought it, you never saw them on the roads, but once you're driving a model, you see it every day. Why? Your RAS is activated and watching for cars that look like yours. Those same cars were always on the road, but you didn't see them because your RAS filtered them out of your awareness so you could focus on other things.

Once you made the purchase, your mind tuned its focus and pointed out each one that crossed your path.

Now imagine what your mind could do if you constantly looked for *opportunities* rather than difficulties or challenges.

When life seems to be caving in on you, it takes constant effort to maintain a positive mindset, but as Albert Einstein said, "In the middle of difficulty lies opportunity."

Here's the positive spin on your worst days: You have survived 100 percent of them. That alone is a win, but there's more to success than survival. The opportunity is to learn and grow and adjust your course of action so the next day, month, and year are better.

If you continue to do what you've always done, you will continue to get what you've always gotten. On the flip side, if you do what you've never done, you will get what you've never gotten. Choose to focus on what you want and move forward with an attitude of gratitude for how far you've come. Ask: *How does what I've learned or experienced equip me to help someone else?*

Stay focused on your goals rather than on your fears. With the right mindset, discipline, and actions, you can make the impossible a reality.

Choose Your Friends Wisely

If you want to kill a big dream, tell it to a small-minded person.

—Steve Harvey

Many of my friends couldn't imagine me doing anything besides working behind the bar, partying all night, chasing girls, and sleeping most of the day. That was their life. Up to that point, it had been mine, too, and they assumed it always would be.

After seeing how Tim and his millionaire friends lived, I was ready to trade in my old life for something more meaningful. Being around people who enjoyed amazing financial success and real relationships made me realize I had bigger and better options than I had ever imagined.

The more time I spent with my new mentors, the more I noticed their code of behavior was completely different from the code my friends lived by. They knew what they wanted and why they wanted it. They knew what their life's purpose was. Rather than living in the moment, they had a plan not just for the night but for the day, week, month, quarter, year—and the next ten years.

Changing your life in a substantial way isn't like flipping a switch. It's rare that you can just walk away from your old life—the habits, hang-ups, toxic relationships, and debt—and never look back. It took me several years to break free from the drug addiction I had developed. It took therapy and even more time to grow emotionally enough to have a healthy relationship with a strong, amazing woman. But it didn't take me long to understand I had a choice and wasn't locked into an average, unfulfilling life.

One of the first intentional steps I took toward greatness was changing who my closest friends were. I didn't cut off all my old friends completely, but I had to pull back. Even now, if someone is into the whole crazy nightlife, I'm going to love him or her from a distance. I might go to lunch with someone who is heavy into the nightlife, but I'm not going to hang out with that person on a regular basis. Our codes of behavior are just too different, and I am determined not to let people whose lives I *don't want* influence mine.

When I changed my environment and started living and working with people I *wanted* to be like, my life took a sharp upward turn. I paid attention to my mentor's code of behavior as I created my own. I also saw firsthand that what Jim Rohn taught is true: "You are the average of the five people you spend the most time with."

I am beyond grateful I found a great mentor. He gave me the plan for success, the most important part of which was working harder on myself than anything else. He poured belief into me when I couldn't see more than a few steps into the future by telling me I had what it took to succeed and I was better than the choices I'd made in the past.

Creating the life I have today certainly hasn't been easy, but all the time and effort was worth it. I know the same will be true for you. Before we close out this chapter, take some time to consider who and what the main influences are in your life. Who is pushing you forward or dragging you back? If someone is dragging you down, how much longer are you going to allow them to have that kind of control over your life? Until you stand up for yourself and break free from that person, it's going to be hard to get to the next level. What messages are you feeding your faith?

When you decide to go for your dreams and start living by a different code, not everyone is going to approve of what you're doing on your journey. Don't be afraid to love people from a distance or even lose a few friends along the way. Do whatever it takes to spend more time with mentors who will pour belief into you. There will be times that fear rocks your world. You'll feel like giving up or turning back. Surrounding yourself with people who encourage you to remember what you want and *why* will give you the strength to stay the course.

What's Your Code?

What do you **believe** about the desires that are currently driving your actions, thoughts, and habits? How are your desires affected by the people in your life?

What desires would help you **become** the best version of yourself?

How does your current **behavior** support your beliefs and desires for your future? How does fear impact your desire? How does your environment, including your relationships, affect your desires?

What behaviors, people, or mindsets **belong** in your code to support positive desire? Given the goals you've set, identify the behaviors, relationships, or mindsets that do not belong in your code of behavior.

Chapter 5
ESSENTIAL 3
DISCIPLINE

Ninety-nine percent of all failures come from people who have a habit of making excuses.

—George Washington Carver

ONE OF MY best friends, Kellen, was on his way from playing college ball to the NFL when his life hit a snag. A stupid mistake took him out of the running for a career in pro ball. Instead of going after the dream he had prepared for throughout high school and college, he ended up working in a corporate job.

He is sharp and has an amazing work ethic, so he quickly climbed up the ladder until he was earning a six-figure salary. The problem was he didn't enjoy his life.

He let societal norms dictate the way he lived. Thinking that what society calls "normal" was the way to gain the wealth he wanted to achieve, he stuck it out in a life that felt average. Like so many people, he had been so hypnotized by the security of health benefits and 401k plans he did stop to consider that he had other—better—options.

He knew how to put in the effort and bring home a paycheck, but his day-to-day work failed to give him joy or a sense of fulfillment.

We've been friends for a long time. He knew me when I was waiting tables in high school and bartending in college, and he has followed my journey from the corporate world to entrepreneurship. The good, bad, ugly, and amazing, he's seen all of it. When he saw the changes that were going on in me, not just in my business but also in my life, he took notice. We talked, and I told him about what I was doing to change my code of behavior. Oh, I didn't use those words at the time, but we talked about the crucial discipline of feeding the mind well. I told him one thing I had to do every day was to tend to my mindset by listening to or reading something inspiring.

Encouraged by the changes in my life, Kellen took a step back to see what he needed to do for himself. What he noticed was what I had been telling him for a long time. He was worth far more to that company than what they were paying him.

He deserved more.

Finally seeing that for himself, Kellen decided to develop the same habit of tending his mindset and started devouring and applying personal development content—reading motivational books and listening to inspirational videos and podcasts. We would talk on the phone for hours about what we were learning. As the inspiration and personal belief took root in his life, he realized he didn't want to keep giving his time and energy to build someone else's dream. He had his own dream.

With the same kind of focused discipline he had applied to his football and corporate careers, my friend made a break from average and launched out on his own. It took a leap of faith and a ton of effort, but, running his own company, he now earns more than double what he brought home from his corporate job.

Starting something new wasn't an easy process. He had to overcome major obstacles to overcome to get his company going. *But he figured it out*! His desire was greater than his excuses, and the result was a winning one. When your excuses are greater than the desire, the result is always a loss. More importantly, he loves what he's doing. He enjoys being the boss, building on his successes, and working on his own schedule. Every day brings new challenges, excitement, and rewards.

The cost of giving into negative desires is negative discipline—a.k.a. bad habits. Remember: Negative desires are the things you want for the wrong reasons. Much of the time, those negative desires are based in fear—fear of rejection, the unknown, and of giving up the fallacy of a secure paycheck. Developing a code of behavior that operates with the perspective of possibility, potential, and optimism often requires a total mindset shift—from fear to faith. Maintaining your new mindset requires discipline in both thought and action, which is why this powerful trait is one of the five essentials for your code of behavior.

Are You Stuck in Average?

Every vice has its excuse ready.

—Publilius Syrus

Average is where most people live, and it's a dangerous place. Average is where complacency rules. The daily grind isn't exciting or fulfilling, but at least it's easy to anticipate.

It's the unknown people tend to fear most, which is why even though few people consciously choose an average life, they end up there by default. They get lulled into believing that paying the bills and living for the weekend and two weeks of vacation a year (if they're lucky) is good enough. It's here in *average* that complacency robs people of their dreams.

Most people, although they are capable of so much more, have a hard time envisioning a different life for themselves. They grew up watching the example of their parents punching the clock. Then, watching their peers, neighbors, and coworkers, they followed the path others had taken. They kept up and went with the flow to maintain the status quo.

It's also what society teaches: Go to school, get the degree, and go work for someone. That's the pattern that people have been taught all their lives. That's exactly what I did.

Working your way up the ladder may give you a false sense of security, but it keeps you on the wrong end of things. Employees don't usually pull into the company parking lot in exotic cars. I'm not saying money is everything, but if you're going to grind your ass off, don't you want the option to buy and do what you want?

Let me emphasize this fact, though: Being successful is not all about money. It doesn't matter where you work or whether you're an employee or an entrepreneur. If you love what you do and you're truly happy, and you wake up with passion and excitement and you have peace of mind, you are doing it right.

The thing about average is it really isn't as easy as it looks. Stress and struggle are par for the course in an average life. Think about it: Could you pay your rent or mortgage next month if you lost your job today? More than half of Americans live paycheck to paycheck. Being out of work for even a couple of weeks would throw their financial lives into chaos.

If you have a few months' worth of expenses in savings, you're doing better than most. But before you feel overly impressed with yourself for being above average, remember this: *Average* is best measured on an individual level. By that, I mean *average* should not be about what anyone else is doing. And it shouldn't be about comparing yourself to the masses. If you look around and think, *I'm doing better than everybody around me*, you aren't using the right measuring stick. (You also need to go back and reread "Choose Your Friends Wisely" in the previous chapter.)

The measuring stick is your potential. What else are you capable of doing?

My friend was earning an above-average salary. Does that mean he should have just settled into a career he didn't love? Should I have said, *Dude, suck it up and just do the work and bring home the paycheck because, hey, it's good enough*?

Of course not!

He wasn't happy because he wasn't living up to his potential, and he knew it. He had so much more in him.

There's that tension again between the present reality and what *could be*.

What about you? If you aren't living up to your full potential, you know it. You can feel that tension between where you are and where you know you could be. Even if you are

69

operating at a higher level than the people around you, you won't feel satisfied if you aren't living at *your* full potential. It may look to others like you're kicking ass, but *you* will know that you still have more in you to give.

Positive discipline is your path out of average. If you ignore that path, you'll keep circling around in an average life—wanting more but never getting there.

The on-ramp to the path of discipline doesn't require an all-terrain vehicle. The truth is if you make consistent, small, intentional changes to your current behavior, you could have an abundant life rather than an average one. Does it take work? Absolutely. But if you will become obsessed with greatness, you will discover the results are so worth the effort.

Get Obsessed with Greatness

Where focus goes, energy flows.

—*Tony Robbins*

Like many things, obsession can be good or bad, positive or negative. Some people get so obsessed with another person they end up with a restraining order against them. Others obsess about how angry they are or how hurt they have been by others that they just can't let those feelings go. When a negative obsession takes over a person's life, it's like drinking poison hoping the other person dies. Resentment, anger, or bitterness consumes their thoughts, dictates their conversations, and controls their lives.

I had a friend who was fascinated by conspiracy theories. He would talk as long as anyone would listen about the government, the pharmaceutical industry, political schemes, pesticides, you name it. He would spend hours scouring the internet for proof of wrongdoing and hidden agendas. Then he would spend hours talking about it. And you know what? Some of the things he would tell me were believable and might have been at least partly true. The problem was his obsession with conspiracies and uncovering the "truth" consumed his thoughts.

He couldn't talk about or focus on anything else. He would get so angry over stories in the news and what other people were doing he couldn't hold a conversation about any other topic. The energy he put into his conspiracy obsession was both disturbing and frustrating.

One day, I'd had enough of his ranting and threw my hands up in exasperation, "Dude, stop thinking about what's bad and what 'they' are doing, and take the energy you're putting toward this and apply it to a business idea and go get successful!"

Immediately he came back at me, telling me I didn't understand. They (whoever "they" happened to be at the moment) were destroying the world in some way.

My response didn't sway him. "Okay, let's say they are. Now what? What are you gonna do about it? If you're gonna do something about it, great. If not, then stop talking about it. Erase it from your mind and focus on what *you* can do in your life right now instead of what someone you don't even know is doing. Remember, 'where energy goes, energy flows.'"

Things have never been the same between us. He couldn't *not* talk about all the things that made him angry, and he wanted to be with people who would be just as obsessed about what was wrong with the world as he was.

That's how we all are when we're obsessed with something. It's hard to shift our focus to anything else. We want to talk about our obsession with others. We want others to talk about it too and get as into it as we are. Our obsessions are

71

the things we think about day and night. And our obsessions can work for us or against us.

Whether they are positive or negative, obsessions produce disciplined behavior. You don't even have to think about being disciplined when you're obsessed with something because everything in you wants to focus your time and attention on that one thing. How many kids do you know who are obsessed with Minecraft or Fortnite or some other video game? It's *all* they can talk about!

For some people, the focus is sports. Other people are obsessed with food or cars or money.

You already know there was a time when my obsessions were women and a good time.

Good or bad, healthy or destructive, wherever you focus your thoughts, time, and emotion is where your energy is going to flow. The good news is you can choose your obsession.

A long time ago, I decided I was going to be obsessed with greatness. I have a standard of excellence for my life in all areas. Whatever I did, I was going to go all in, 100 percent. When I got into weight training, I became obsessed with my physique—burning off fat and building muscle. When I started my business, I obsessed about getting better every day in the work I needed to do to succeed. My obsessions almost automatically changed my focus and my behaviors. I became disciplined about whatever would move me toward my goals because I was obsessed with achieving them.

Some people live with a mindset of "all things in moderation." That's not my take on life, and it's not how you achieve great things. What if, instead of living in mediocre moderation, you chose to cut out the activities that didn't serve you well and focused your attention on what it would take to make your life truly great or to make your dreams a reality? What if you became obsessed with excellence in the areas of life that matter most to you? In *Be Obsessed or Be Average*, Grant Cardone makes a powerful case for positive obsession:

> *Imagine if every person on earth threw themselves fully and completely into their positive obsessions without reservation, regret, or apology. Overnight the world would be a better place. With everyone so focused on their own production and creating their own success, there would be no time for war, drugs, or other wasteful, unnecessary destruction. We'd all hit levels of success previously thought impossible—and inspire one another to do more and be more.*

You, too, must decide what you're going to allow to consume your mind and drive your actions. What are you obsessed with? How is that obsession impacting your behavior?

The Key to Greatness

Without self-discipline, success is impossible, period.

—Lou Holtz

Discipline is what takes us from knowledge to action—from excuses to results. Without it, we get stuck. Even if we have a great goal and all the information we need to make it a reality, without the discipline to move us to action, we won't make any progress.

Positive discipline moves you in the right direction, just like negative discipline moves you in the wrong direction.

After high school, I didn't have the right kind of discipline. I was great at hanging out with friends, partying, and watching television all day. I dropped out of community college because I didn't have a clue what I wanted to do with my life.

Between the ages of twenty-one and twenty-three, my buddy John and I worked together doing door-to-door sales. We actually did really well for a while. The company we were working for assigned us a territory to cover, and initially, we made plenty of sales and earned decent commissions. Because we were confined to that assigned area, we eventually ran out of leads. After more than ten months of no new leads (and no new sales), we were broke. We quit that job, and, at twenty-three, I moved back in with my mom. John tagged along.

In return for a free place to live, we promised my mom we would help out around the house and not eat all her groceries. We had good intentions, but when my mom left for work each day, we were still sleeping off the party from the night before. When she got home from work, she would find us lounging in the pool or playing video games while the house was a mess—and we messed it up.

It went on like that for a while. After a couple of months, John ended up going to Houston to do door-to-door sales again. I decided I would stay and go back to school. Unfortunately, my self-discipline didn't improve after John left.

Finally, Mom had enough and kicked me out. I deserved it.

I was a young adult with the intelligence and ability to earn a living wage. What I didn't have was the discipline to do anything other than party, lie by the pool, or play video games.

My mom has always been in my corner. Both my parents have. I have been blessed that way.

The courage it took to kick me out was proof of both her love and belief in me.

Of course, it didn't feel like that at the time. At the time, I was angry. But deep down, I knew I didn't really *want* to live in my mom's house forever. Even back then, I knew I wanted something great for my life. I just hadn't figured out what it was yet.

I moved out and found myself working job to job with one being a personal trainer at a gym, before I decided to go back to school. This is when I earned my business degree from the University of North Texas. To pay my bills, I tended bar a few nights every week. Little by little, I started to understand the power of setting a goal and working every day to achieve it. It was self-discipline in its infancy.

Several years later, when I began my journey of entrepreneurship, I made intentional personal development one of my habits or disciplines, and it's one I maintain to this day. I go to events to hear speakers share their stories and best practices for success. I participate in coaching calls and mastermind groups that challenge me to stretch further and reach higher. I intentionally surround myself with people who have what I want so I can learn from their example. I am constantly reading and listening to books that challenge me to improve.

I do all that because I have learned my success in any area of life—from my relationships to my business goals to my income—depends on the health and strength of my mindset. The mind is a muscle. And just like a muscle, if you don't work your mind, it'll get weak. I know if I slip on my mental discipline, I'll get weak and negative, and my results will drop from excellent to average.

Here's the truth: Your paycheck will always match your mindset. If your mindset drops, your income will drop to match it. You've heard the stories about lottery winners who go bankrupt after winning big, right? Their mindset couldn't handle the millionaire status. They should have followed Jim Rohn's advice: "If someone hands you a million dollars, best you become a millionaire, or you won't get to keep the money."

To live your best life, you have to become your best self—from the inside out.

Mindset, knowledge, and action work together to produce results. You need the right attitude to keep you striving toward your unimaginable goals. Without it, you'll get discouraged and give up when you hit a roadblock.

You also need knowledge. Too many people operate from the mentality that what they don't know won't hurt them. That's a lie! What you don't know can and does hurt. It's knowledge that helps you vibrate at a higher frequency—when you're thinking big. It's this kind of thinking that attracts new and different types of people and conversations that leads to greater opportunities. Get the knowledge you need to succeed! Be willing to ask questions and seek out answers from people who have already made it to where you want to be. It's not a sign of weakness to not know all the answers. It's a sign of weakness to act like you know everything and to try and do everything yourself. One of my biggest shifts to success was the art of delegation.

Lastly, you must take action. The right information won't help you if you don't put it to work. Motivational speaker and author Eric Thomas says it this way: "Knowledge isn't power. *Applied* knowledge is power." It doesn't matter how much you know if you don't put it into action.

If any one of those three elements is off for you, you won't get the results you want:

- If your mindset is one of victim or self-defeat, it's unlikely you will take the actions you need to move toward any positive goals. You might manage survival or even average, but not greatness.

- If your mindset is crazy optimistic but you lack the right knowledge, you might not know the *right* actions to take. If your activity level is high but you're doing the wrong things, you can be the hardest worker in the room and never make it where you want to go. (This truth gets even harder to swallow if all your energy is focused on building someone else's dream and they decide when, if, and how far you can climb up the corporate ladder.)

- If your mindset is positive and you know what to do to achieve your goal, you still have to follow up with consistent action. Without action, you'll just feel great about going nowhere!

It's easy to get tripped up at any one of these three stages. The remedy, often, is discipline. You need discipline to feed your mind positive content on a regular basis. You need discipline to learn from mentors, books, and other resources to acquire the knowledge necessary for your success. And you need discipline to take the action that will move you toward your goals.

I've learned the hard way that the need for discipline never subsides.

After I had been building my business for a few years, I eased up on some of the things I'd been so disciplined about. I thought I had enough experience and enough success that I could just coast for a bit. I had achieved some of my major goals and was earning six figures annually. My business ran, at least to a degree, on autopilot, and it brought in more money than I needed every month, even if I put in very little time.

I took a break from pretty much everything. In a sense, I was back to being that twenty-one-year-old kid hanging out at the pool all day, except for this time, I had money coming in every month and didn't have to deal with the stress of being broke. If I wanted to party, I could fund my own bad habits.

If I wanted to do nothing but lie around and watch Netflix, I could. I guess I thought I could get away with it because I had this image of being successful, but the people closest to me noticed the change in me almost immediately.

My mom called. "Jason, I just want to check on you. Are you okay?" she asked. I tried to brush her off. "I'm good," I assured her.

It was a lie. When I was home, I would sit around watching television—doing nothing. That kind of behavior wasn't normal for me anymore. It hadn't been normal for me since I had started my business.

A few days later, one of my team members called me. Sounding concerned, he said, "Dude, where've you been? Are you doing okay?"

"Never better, man!" I told him.

"Man, come on, bro. You're not showing up, and we need you around. Step it up, man. Come on!"

I brushed him off, telling him I'd see him soon.

A few days later, I had dinner with my mom. Clearly, I hadn't convinced her that things were fine because she kept asking what was going on with me. The thing was, she saw how my energy had dropped.

She heard it in my voice the next time we talked on the phone too. "Jason, I feel like something is off with you," she said. She went on to remind me of the dedication I'd shown to my health during my bodybuilding competitions. I had to laugh. She was right. A couple years earlier, I had gone to my great-grandmother's birthday celebration, which happened to fall right in the middle of competition season. I was living off vegetables and lean protein—watching every bite—and there I was at a big family get-together with all kinds of good food, including birthday cake. Talk about torture. (I hung out in the back room to avoid the worst of the temptation!)

"You're one of the most disciplined people I know," my mom reminded me. "If you could put that same kind of discipline toward your life and career, there's nothing you couldn't do."

She was right, of course. Self-doubt consumed the optimism I usually felt about life. I felt drained and weighed down—even though I really didn't have a reason to be. At first, I tried to play the victim as if something had happened *to* me. The truth was, I had stopped doing what I loved. Rather than being actively engaged in my life and business, I had pulled back from other people and from the activities and mindset habits that energized me.

Not long after that, I went to a seminar to hear two of my favorite business speakers. In one of the presentations, the word *discipline* kept coming up. The speaker talked about the fact that we are all disciplined in the things we really care about. We make time for what is most important to us.

Discipline.

I couldn't escape it!

The truth is, I didn't want to. I knew what it felt like to live with this trait working for me—and against me. I understood firsthand that if you're not growing, you're dying. Discipline was what had helped me grow my business. More importantly, it was what made *me* grow—made me stronger mentally and physically. Without it, that growth stopped, and life started moving in the wrong direction.

When I set some new goals and reengaged with a renewed commitment to discipline in not only my actions but also my mindset, my life improved almost instantly.

Positivity Is on Purpose

In this world you're either growing or you're dying,
so get in motion and grow.

—Lou Holtz

Peter Hernandez's childhood was anything but average—or easy. His parents were musicians and earned a living performing for tourists at Las Vegas-style venues on Waikiki Beach in Honolulu, Hawaii. It wasn't long before Peter joined his parents on stage. At just four years old, he knew how to make the crowds love him. Night after night, for six years, he stole the show with his Elvis impression. Lights, music, and adoring fans were a way of life for Peter and his family. "It was just this kind of razzle-dazzle lifestyle," he says.

When he was twelve, that *razzle-dazzle* life took a sharp turn. His parents divorced and split the family. His sisters lived with his mom, and he and his brother lived with his dad.

Divorce is never easy, especially on the kids, but life got a whole lot tougher when the gigs dried up and the money ran out. Without money or a place to live, the boys and their dad were homeless for a time and ended up living in an abandoned bird sanctuary named Paradise Park, where his dad had worked before it closed. They lived together in one room with one bed—and no bathroom except for the one across the park.

Rather than remembering that time in his life as a series of hard blows, Peter, whom you may know better as Bruno Mars, says it was one of the best times of his life. In an interview on *60 Minutes*, he said, "We had each other, and it never felt like it was the end of the world." No matter what the challenge was or what they lacked, Mars says his mindset stayed locked on two things. First, they had each other. Second, the situation, however bad, was temporary and they could and would figure out a solution.

The belief that the difficulties were temporary rather than destined or permanent and they could figure out the next steps helped them survive. They lived there for two years while he and his family got back on their feet. That same attitude stuck with him as he found his own way in the music industry. It kept him focused on solutions rather than problems. "Maybe that's why I have this mentality when it comes to the music. 'Cause I know I'm gonna figure it out, just give me some time," he told the interviewer.

Mars left Hawaii, determined to make a name for himself in music, but the hits just kept on coming—and not the good kind. Motown Records signed him in 2004 and then dropped him a year later. To Mars, it seemed like no one understood him. He says his mixed heritage threw people off: "He's not black enough. He's not white enough. He's got a Latin last name, but he doesn't speak Spanish." And his music, which his childhood stage experiences had infused with rock and roll, reggae, hip hop, and rhythm and blues, didn't easily fit into any category. Label executives and marketers were confused: "Who are we selling this to? Are you making urban music? Are you making pop music? What kind of music are you making?" But bottom line, he says, "I wasn't ready yet."

It took time, but he figured out the music business. He partnered with mentors and wrote songs for other musicians until, at twenty-four, his single "Just the Way You Are" rose to the top of the charts. Things should have been perfect, but all the struggles and extreme success at a young age took its toll. In September 2010, Las Vegas police busted Mars for cocaine possession.

He has since called that arrest a reality check. He pleaded guilty for possession and ended up with 200 hours of community service and a $2,000 fine. He was also required to take a drug counseling course. Once again, he figured things out and got his life and career back on track.

To date, Mars has sold more than 180 million singles and is one of the bestselling music artists of all time. The album he released in late 2021 with collaborator Anderson .Paak, "An Evening with Silk Sonic," surpassed a billion streams on Spotify in January 2022. Mars, who chose the name because he has always been shooting for the stars, continues to be dedicated to his craft.

Mars is an inspiration to me for many reasons, and one of them is his incredible discipline. Another is his willingness to persevere. He didn't let the dream killers stop him from going after what he wanted. He doesn't quit until he gets the details right—from the words and music to the choreography and presence he brings to the stage. His discipline is what helps him put on a killer show. I saw him in Dallas at the American Airlines Center in October 2018. That show is still one of my favorite concerts.

Another thing that shows up again and again in his story is his mindset. The man chooses to stay positive, to learn from his mistakes as well as from his successes, to keep moving forward, and to figure it out. I love that he calls his memories from the time he spent living in an abandoned bird zoo "the best" because he was able to focus on what he had instead of what he didn't. That's a great example of having an attitude of gratitude and goes back to the truth that positivity is a choice.

That kind of mindset doesn't develop naturally or by accident. Happiness is a choice. Positivity is on purpose. Your mindset doesn't have to be determined by your circumstances or your failures. You can choose your focus. You can choose your obsession. You can choose to be disciplined in the things that move you in the direction you want to go. And you can always choose happiness no matter the current situation, knowing that wherever you are is temporary.

But you have to choose.

Challenges are everywhere. Disappointments are inescapable. Hits—and not the good kind—are a part of life. It's going to feel natural to get down on yourself or be angry with your circumstances from time to time, even if you know *you* created them. Negative thoughts will pound you with self-doubt and depreciation. You can't always control the thoughts that come *into* your mind, but you can control how long they *stay* there.

Choose your focus.

Focus on what you can do. Focus on figuring it out— whatever "it" is for you at the moment.

Remember: Positivity gets you much further than negativity. Discipline your mind. Keep it positive. When you pair the right mindset with the right actions—consistently, not just when you feel like it—victory is inevitable.

What's Your Code?

What do you **believe** about your ability to be disciplined?

What disciplines would it take for you to **become** the best version of yourself?

Does your current **behavior** support your beliefs and desires for your future?

Which disciplines do you need to replace, and which ones **belong** in your code of behavior?

Chapter 6
ESSENTIAL 4
CONFIDENCE

Believe in yourself! Have faith in your abilities!
Without a humble but reasonable confidence in your
own powers, you cannot be successful or happy.

—Norman Vincent Peale

WHEN TOM BRADY announced his retirement in January 2022, social media lit up with GOAT memes and well wishes. Brady ended his football career with the respect of fans worldwide and has been dubbed by many, including his former New England Patriots' coach, Bill Belichick, as the "best player in NFL history." In his twenty-two years playing pro ball, he shattered records with the most touchdown passes (624) and most passing yards (84,250) in the league.

Earning seven Lombardi trophies and five Super Bowl Most Valuable Player awards, he also earned the respect of his team.

The celebratory footage popping up in the news at his retirement focuses primarily on those great moments. If you only watched the highlights, it would be easy to assume Brady's success came easily.

Nothing could be further from the truth. The reality is his success on and off the field is the result of intense physical and mental work and dedication.

Brady's high school football coach, Bob Vinal, believed the young player had potential early on. It wasn't Brady's speed (he was considered a slow runner) or his stature (he was lanky and fit, but not muscular) that impressed his coach. It was his character the coach appreciated. "When that guy puts his mind to something, he's pretty driven," Vinal said in the documentary on Brady's life, *Becoming the GOAT*. Starting as a backup quarterback on the junior varsity team for his high school in San Mateo, California, he had to work his way up the roster. His dedication to improvement included watching game film every weekend with his teammates so they could better understand what worked and what didn't. He sought help from his coach when he hit walls, and he developed an intense training regimen above and beyond the school's program.

His sweat and persistence paid off, and by his senior year, he was honored as an All-State and All-Far West performer. He had his pick of colleges across the nation and took a scholarship to the University of Michigan. Once again, he was starting at the bottom as a red-shirt freshman, and once again, he found people who helped him grow. This time, in addition to the coaching staff and first-string players he prac-ticed with, it was Greg Harden, the counselor who worked with Michigan's student athletes, who helped him move past some of his self-imposed mental limits and find his stride as a solid player on the team. It wasn't until his senior year that he had the opportunity to start, but even then, he shared the role of starting quarterback with another player.

Brady practiced and played hard because he wanted to go pro, and there was at least one team watching him. Although he had improved his game significantly throughout his college career, his stats weren't all that impressive. He still wasn't the fastest (in fact, he was one of the slowest quarterbacks in the 2000 draft). Coaches also doubted he had the strength and accuracy to throw deep.

A scout from the New England Patriots, however, saw the same thing Brady's high school coach had seen in him all those years ago: character. He was a hard worker, a leader, and a team player who was coachable. The scout told the coaching staff Brady would be a good mental fit for the team. After doing his research, Belichick agreed Brady had a mindset that would serve the team well. The problem was the Patriots didn't need a quarterback at the time.

What a hit it must have been to Brady's confidence when team after team passed him over in the first round—and then the second, third, fourth, and fifth rounds of the 2000 draft. Finally, in the sixth round, the Patriots' staff noticed the player they had liked all along was still up for grabs and signed him. He was number 199 out of 254 draftees that year.

With Drew Bledsoe as the Patriots' starting quarterback, Brady spent all but one of the games his first season on the sidelines, again having to prove his ability to contribute. He didn't wait, however, to make himself and his intention for greatness known. When he met Bob Kraft, the team's owner, he told him, "I'm the best decision this franchise has ever made." Those aren't words anyone would expect from a new player—and a sixth-round draft pick at that—but it turned out to be true.

When Brady finally got the chance to play in his second season with the Patriots, he made the most of it and never looked back. Covering for Bledsoe, who had experienced a life-threatening injury, Brady led the team to a Super Bowl win in 2001. It was the first of his ten Super Bowl games with the Patriots.

Brady played twenty years for the Patriots. After a 2021 Superbowl win for the Tampa Bay Buccaneers, Brady announced his retirement in January 2022—and forty days later changed his mind, saying he had unfinished business on the field. Evidently, he's not ready to quit just yet. Even if you aren't a fan of the Patriots or the Buccaneers, Brady's accomplishments, earned through years of hard work and a don't-quit, always-improve mindset, are undeniably impressive.

Never Trust a Thief

We won't be distracted by comparison if we are captivated with purpose.

—Bob Goff

When I woke up in the cardiac intensive care unit after flatlining, I felt grateful to be alive. So few people survive a widow-maker heart attack with a 100 percent blockage, and there I was back home in my high-rise apartment in Austin three days later with no damage to my heart. With my heart pumping like normal, it was as if the heart attack had never happened.

Gratitude washed over me, and, man, joy for being alive was all I felt for a while. Nothing—from the clothes in my closet to the things I had been worried about a few weeks earlier—seemed important anymore. *I was alive!* That's what mattered.

Life carried me on a high like that for a while. I kept working, building my business, taking care of my health and my family, and I was happy. After several months, though, the shine wore off a bit. Don't get me wrong. I was (*am*) still happy to be alive. With enough distance between death and my daily life, however, I started looking around and paying attention to what others were doing. Specifically, I started noticing others' successes. One friend had recently purchased a plane—with cash—and was, at twenty-eight years old, earning more than $2 million *a month*. Another one of my buddies was crushing it in real estate and making multimillion-dollar deals, and the list goes on. These people are killing it!

I knew better than to compare myself to others. I *knew* even then that comparison is the thief of joy, but I did it anyway.

Before I realized what was happening, comparison stole my joy for being alive and successful in my own right. *Man, I should be so much farther ahead*, I thought. I kept thinking along those lines and started to get depressed. My mom and Ana, my girlfriend, both noticed the shift in my attitude and asked me about it. When I explained I was frustrated because my life hadn't moved as fast or as far as I thought it should have, they called me on it.

I was on the phone with my mom, telling her I was irritated because I wasn't where I wanted to be. My mom immediately pointed out how much I had grown and accomplished during the past few years. I had come so far—mind, body, and spirit. So much had changed for me, from becoming a successful entrepreneur to kicking my drug addiction to making a real difference in people's lives with my speaking and training.

Ana stared me down and pointed out the obvious when I shared my frustration with her.

"Just a few months ago, you were simply grateful to be alive and breathing. And now you're not happy?"

Both of them had me, and I knew it.

I had allowed comparison to take a swing at my confidence. The hit connected and had temporarily stolen my happiness.

Can you relate? Are you looking around at what others are doing and thinking, *What's wrong with me? Why am I not further along?*

The pursuit of big goals is a good thing, but if we're always wishing for the next thing, assuming it will make us happy, we will *never* be happy. Happiness isn't about the future. It's about the present, otherwise we're always chasing it. Besides that, basing our success or happiness on what others have achieved is futile—and with social media today, it's so easy to do.

Now, listen, I don't hate social media. I have my own accounts and have used them as a way to get to know about people and even to make some connections that have turned into real-life relationships and business deals. But social media isn't real life. People post their greatest moments, the best pictures, the final result. What you don't see is what's going on behind the scenes.

Shortly before this book went to press, Cheslie Kryst, a former Miss USA winner, took her own life. Her tragic death shocked even the people closest to her. If you were to look at her Instagram account, you would assume this intelligent, beautiful young woman had everything. What her social media presence didn't show, however, was the pain of depression she suffered from daily.

Ten months before her death, she wrote an essay for *Allure. com* that highlights how the need to measure up affects people you might assume would be immune to the comparison trap. She pushed herself to achieve from an early age and said that before she won the Miss USA title at age twenty-eight, the striving left her feeling empty. "Too often, I noticed that the only people impressed by an accomplishment were those who wanted it for themselves. Meanwhile, I was rewarded with a lonely craving for the next award. Some would see this hunger and label it 'competitiveness'; others might call it the unquenchable thirst of insecurity."

After she won the pageant crown, she felt a renewed sense of purpose. She had earned a spot on a platform that would allow her to use her voice to speak out against injustice. Unfortunately, that crown made her a target. She wrote: "My challenge of the status quo certainly caught the attention of the trolls, and I can't tell you how many times I have deleted comments on my social media pages that had vomit emojis and insults telling me I wasn't pretty enough to be Miss USA or that my muscular build was actually a 'man body.'

"And that was just my looks. My opinions, on the other hand, were enough to make a traditional pageant fan clutch their pearls."

My point is here is two-fold: First, we let comparison rob us of our joy when the pictures we're comparing ourselves to don't show the whole story. Many times, even the people who seem to have it all aren't as happy as we might think. Like Cheslie Kryst, they may be dealing with challenges, like depression, behind the scenes.

Second: When we make life about keeping up with what others have or living in constant pursuit of "what's next," we will never be content. It is *good* to go after your dreams—huge dreams. Just make sure they are yours and that you've chosen them for reasons that are meaningful to *you*.

Refuse to let comparison rob you of your joy or tear down your confidence.

Stay focused on *your* goals and *your* why. Develop an attitude of gratitude. Be thankful for what is right in front of you. As Jim Rohn said, "Learn how to be happy with what you have while you pursue all that you want."

Attract Success

Success is something you attract by the person you become.

—Jim Rohn

Comedian, actor, and CEO of Laugh Out Loud Network Kevin Hart says that, in some ways, that "pursuit of all you want"—and life itself—is like a game. "It's a game. This thing is serious, but it's got a game-like quality to it. This thing called life," he said during a podcast interview on *The Joe Rogan Experience*. "And that doesn't mean that you play with it. Understand what I'm saying here. It means that you can do what you put your mind to. And if you continue to put your mind to it, the game opens up new levels."

Every new level boosts not only your success but your confidence as well—which leads to new opportunities, more success, and greater confidence. "You get a new level, and each new level that gets opened up, you're able to adapt a different mindset and a different approach," Hart said. "You can stop at that level, or you can go, 'I want more levels.'"

The question is this: Do you want to stop, or do you want to level up? When Hart is faced with that question he asks, "What's my reason not to go after everything that I possibly can?"

In other words, why not? Why wouldn't I go for it?

Why wouldn't anyone go for it?

For me, personally, leveling up is the only answer when it comes to my relationships, my career, and my finances. One thing I've learned along the way is every new level demands more—more authenticity, more discipline, and more intentionality. You can't get to the next place you want to go by thinking the same old thoughts or falling back on the same old habits. That's why Jim Rohn's quote hits home for me: "Success is something you attract by the person you become." You and I only thrive when we are constantly growing and becoming more than we were yesterday.

To attract the success you want, you have to become the kind of person who can handle that success, and you can't fake who you are. You've heard the old saying, right? "Fake it till you make it." Faking it may fool the onlookers, but *you* will know if you're being honest with others and yourself. You will know if you're acting with integrity.

Several years ago, I learned it's impossible to maintain integrity with people if you're being fake with them. I had been building my business for a couple of years and had learned significant lessons from so many excellent people. One mentor, in particular, had been crucial in my journey. This man had my respect on every level. He was incredibly successful in his business and had an amazing marriage and great relationships with his kids. Everyone who knew him loved him, including me. I would call him for advice or just to get his perspective on different situations, and he never failed to steer me in the right direction.

This mentor had a full plate but was always ready to encourage people who were willing to do the work. He respected people who respected themselves. On the flip side of that coin, he didn't have much patience or time for people who chose to knowingly dive headfirst into bad relationships and situations. He wasn't above helping anyone, but he had high expectations for the people he worked with. If you knew what you were supposed to be doing and chose to sabotage your own success just for fun, he wasn't going to waste his time trying to convince you otherwise. I know that about him because that's exactly what I did.

My journey out of drug addiction wasn't a straight path. It was more like a winding trail that circled back on itself and went off into a dark valley before turning back to the healthier side of life. I can look back now and see whenever I headed in the wrong direction, I was traveling with the wrong people.

I'd been doing well, but somewhere along the way, I linked back up with an old girlfriend. Our relationship was toxic the first time, and the second time around, it wasn't any better.

I also knew my mentor wouldn't approve of the relationship or my drug use. Afraid he would judge me, or worse than that, stop mentoring me, I hid my drug use from him. Each time we talked, he would open the conversation by asking how I was doing, and every time, I purposely left out anything he wouldn't approve of. My life was threatening to spiral completely out of control, but with my mentor, I pretended everything was fine. I didn't want him to think less of me, so I decided to fake it. Rather than admit I was in trouble and needed help, I lied and told him I was good, business was good, everything was good.

As a rule, people don't like to be lied to, and my mentor was no exception. Several people knew what I was up to, and when the truth got back to him, he cut off communication with me. The next time I texted him, my message wouldn't deliver. I tried calling a few times, but every call went straight to voicemail. It didn't take long to figure out he had blocked me—and it was my own fault. I knew his expectations, and I had fallen short.

The thought of losing that relationship devastated me, so when I saw him at a business event, I stopped him and asked if we could talk. I offered to buy him lunch and told him I knew I'd done something to upset him and wanted the chance to make things right.

He agreed to talk with me and told me word had gotten back to him about the kinds of choices I was making with my life. He told me that, at first, he hadn't wanted to believe what people were saying. When he heard the same kinds of things from enough people, he finally accepted the truth. That's when he blocked me.

He didn't tell me who said what, and I didn't ask. I also didn't know exactly what he knew or didn't know, but right then and there, I opened up to him and told him everything. I told him I wasn't proud of my behavior. I was in a dark place. I made no excuses. I owned my behavior and the consequences, and I apologized for being dishonest with him.

Owning my mistakes and not making excuses was the key for him. He told me he appreciated my honesty and said, "I wish you would have been honest with me all along."

My mentor told me he didn't expect perfection, but he did expect me to be straight with him. I had broken his trust and lost his respect by lying to him. It devastated me to know I had disappointed him.

The truth was I had let us both down, and, in doing so, my self-confidence took a hit. Jumping back into a toxic relationship had been a huge mistake. Trying to hide that part of my life from him only made me feel worse about myself. I had lied to him because I hadn't wanted to lose him as a mentor—which was exactly what happened anyway. The moral of that story? Be upfront and honest, even if you're afraid of the outcome.

I had come a long way in a couple years. In that time, I had gotten a glimpse at what was possible for my life. After I found the courage to get real with my mentor, I realized I had almost lost everything by sliding back into my old code of behavior. It took a while for things to improve in my life. I eventually ended the relationship with the woman I should never have gotten involved with (again). I got back on the path, headed in the right direction. This time, because I was no longer lying to him, my mentor walked along with me to help me stay on that path.

Many people try to fake success because they think it makes them look good. They have this false idea of what success is, so they try to act or look like someone else. Meanwhile, their self-doubt grows behind that mask. They feel like they can never measure up to what they see around them. They also fear losing people's respect and admiration if and when the world figures out their image is a thin, easily breakable shell.

You don't need to fake it. Get to the work of becoming a *better you*. That's how you will attract the success you want.

You can't be inauthentic and attract real success. Life doesn't work that way long term.

It's only when you focus on becoming *the best version of you* that you can truly step into your own greatness. You don't need to fake it. Get to the work of becoming a *better you*. That's how you will attract the success you want.

Faith + Action

Luck is when determination meets opportunity.

—Richard Branson

Gosh, you're so lucky.

I've lost count of the number of times I've heard that. Whether it's from someone from my past who knew me "way back when" or from someone I've just met, it always makes me laugh. My success has nothing to do with luck and everything to do with a mindset of faith and intentional action.

Too many people wait for good things to just fall into place. When something good happens to themselves or others, they act surprised or dismiss it as a coincidence. These same people show their envy of others' "luck" with statements like these:

"He was just in the right place at the right time. I have never been lucky."

"Some people have all the luck, and I'm not one of them."

In my experience, the real key to success is the combination of faith and action. Faith plus action is what attracts success.

That combination of mindset and effort—faith plus action—puts you in control of what happens in your life. No, you can't control every circumstance in your life, but what you think about it and what you do with it shapes the outcome.

When you see yourself as worthy of greatness and believe in possibilities for a successful future, you will do things that align with that potential. In other words, you will take action on your belief, and you're far more likely to experience better outcomes as a result. It's not coincidence or luck. It's faith plus action. Here are a few real-life examples that illustrate my belief:

I believe am alive for a reason. When I had that widow-maker heart attack, I didn't go into that emergency clinic thinking I was going to die. I had faith I would be okay. Some people may call that being naive, but scientific research shows a positive mindset is beneficial to a person's health—and specifically heart health.

I had already survived a heart attack and believed I would survive this one. My mindset wouldn't let me dwell on the negative possibilities. I believe my faith played a huge part in my survival and recovery, but so did the fact that I listened to my body and got help when I needed it. Faith plus action.

Even before the heart attack, my health habits of exercising regularly and nourishing my body well had created the condition of physical strength. Even as my heart struggled, my body responded in a way that prevented permanent damage. That's a major factor in why I am alive and well today. My positive mindset is another contributing condition to my survival.

The mind is powerful!

If I had believed I was going to die that day, my mind might have given my body permission to call it quits. But I believed I had a lot to live for and that my time wasn't up yet.

I believe relationships are important. Relationships take work! Whether it's with a partner or spouse, your parents, other family members, friends, or business partners, I've learned I can't neglect the relationships I cherish. Showing up authentically, being loyal, caring about people, setting boundaries, and working on myself are all actions that create the conditions for healthy connections with others.

I believe I am worthy of success. Success is the result of having the faith to set big, purposeful goals and then applying the right actions and focused discipline. It's also a result of maintaining a mindset that there are new opportunities for success *everywhere.*

Here's how I intentionally attract success:

- Combining positive belief (faith) with the right actions.

- Working on myself.

- Studying people.

- Pouring into people.

- Encouraging people and getting them to understand they have more worth than they think.

- Lifting people up and telling them how great they are, how capable they are, and everything they're not used to hearing.

You can attract success by being intentional with your mindset, your words, your actions, and your interactions with others. Often it will take hard work, and the right actions are a simple choice we can make every day:

- *Smile at people and compliment people generously.* It doesn't cost you a dime to make someone feel good about themselves. It's amazing how a friendly face and a kind word can open doors. One of my mentors always encouraged me to pour into others whenever I was feeling down. The effect was powerful. As humans, we feel our best when we are doing good and helping others.

- *Lift people up!* Strong people lift others up. Weak people tear others down. People need your strength and encouragement.

- *Show respect and treat **everyone** with kindness.* No matter who you're talking to, from the CEO to the janitor, treat other people with the same respect. The way you treat people says a lot about you and the way you think about yourself.

- *Be curious about others.* Showing genuine interest in others will draw people to you.

They will want to spend time with you. Whenever you meet someone, ask open-ended questions that invite them to talk about themselves—what they do for a living, what their interests are, and what challenges they're facing. People's favorite topic is themselves! So, rather than trying to be interesting, be interested! What you discover about the other person may reveal an opportunity that would benefit both of you.

- *Be a problem solver.* People have plenty of problems, and they don't need you or anyone else adding to the long list of things that need to be fixed. Rather than complaining about problems, come up with solutions.

- *Focus on winning!* The Law of Attraction says our thoughts draw things to us. If your thoughts are focused on all the bad things that could happen, more of those things will show up in your life. If you focus on what you *want* to happen, you're far more likely to manifest those positive opportunities. (For some quick insight on the Law of Attraction, read *The Secret* by Rhonda Byrne.)

These ideas may sound too simple, but I promise you, they work. You never know when the next opportunity for incredible success will walk into your life, so you always have to be ready to receive it.

Right before the New Year, a guy came into my shop with his little girl. We had a great talk while his daughter had a ball playing with the Christmas decorations we had put up for the season. We gave her bells from the decorations, as well as every color straw she wanted. We had talked for about twenty minutes when, because I'm curious, I asked what he did for a living. Turns out, he was the head of nutrition for one of the nation's largest college football programs.

I have several businesses, and one of them happens to be in the health and wellness industry. Nutrition is what that business is all about. You can imagine how a connection with someone who oversees the nutrition for an entire football program might open some very profitable opportunities for me. Who knows, right?

We talked for a while longer while his little girl played. I told her she could just keep the decorations she'd been playing with. As they left, I invited him to come back soon.

That night, I got an Instagram message from the guy who said his daughter had liked the bells so much she had fallen asleep holding them. He thanked me for our hospitality and said he had enjoyed the conversation and appreciated the way we had treated his daughter. He also noted genuine hospitality is rare these days—especially in the busyness of the holiday shopping season.

Here's the thing: The hospitality we showed and the way we were with his daughter that day is the way we do business every day. (Remember what I said about treating everyone with respect and kindness? You never know who you might be talking to!) I had no idea who he was when he came into my store. Someone else might have been bugged to have a toddler running around the shop and playing with the decorations. We truly didn't mind at all. I was happy we could keep her occupied so her dad could just hang out and talk for a while. And my curiosity is authentic. It's just me being me. I want everyone who comes into my store to leave knowing we genuinely care about them.

He has come back to my shop often since his first visit, and I'm enjoying getting to know him better. I still have no idea whether our connection will lead to additional business. (If it does, I'm sure somebody will say I got lucky.) What I do know is, if I hadn't created the right conditions with a great shop and taken the right actions by delivering genuine hospitality, he wouldn't have felt welcomed on his first visit and never would have written me that note or come back into the store.

Choose Your Seat

You don't have to sit in the back.
You can work your ass off and choose your seat.

—SuperMario McKinley

Success builds on success. Every repeated thought and action shapes the way you think about yourself and your potential.

- When you pay attention to what you have (instead of falling into the comparison trap), you notice you have more to be grateful for than you might have imagined.

- When you live authentically while working to improve yourself and your results, you don't have to fake anything because who you become is a better version of your true self.

- When you treat *all* people well and are open to new opportunities, more of those opportunities find you more often.

That quote from my buddy SuperMario about choosing your seat is all about creating the right conditions for success—and for improving your confidence. The average person doesn't think of that when they buy a seat on a plane or at the ballpark. Most people just go for the cheapest seats. But you aren't average. You don't have to sit in the nosebleed section at the football stadium or in economy class on a flight. You can choose your seat—first class, front and center, box seats, or balcony. You aren't relegated to the cheap seats.

"I don't have that kind of money!" That's the objection, right? The best seats in the house, regardless of the venue, are going to cost more. The thing to consider is whether those seats are worth the extra money.

Well, let's see. When you sit in first class on an airplane, the seats are comfortable and offer plenty of space to stretch out, which means you can rest on the flight and arrive at your destination looking and feeling rested. If you need to work, the table space is big enough for your laptop or tablet *and* your drink. In econo-class, you'll be lucky if your laptop fits on the tiny table, especially if the guy in front of you decides to lean back in his seat.

The difference in comfort is enough to make you want to shell out the extra bills for the first-class seat, but comfort isn't the best reason. I always fly first class. I'm six-foot-one, so the extra legroom is nice, but that's not why I'm willing to pay more for my seat. I fly first class for a few reasons:

1. I like the advantage of checking in at the priority line which is always shorter.

2. I like getting on the airplane first because I know there will be a place for my carry on.

3. I like getting my bags first.

4. I like the service at first class.

5. I like the bathroom close because I drink at least a gallon of water a day.

6. I also like being around the caliber of people who sit in first class.

It's the same reason I get a suite when I go to a ball game or buy front and center or lower-level seats at a concert. I know I'll get the best experience, and I'll increase my odds of meeting other success-focused people.

I took up golf for the same reason. The conversations in the clubhouse or between holes have led to better relationships with people I respect. While we play, I listen and learn and glean new insights about business and life. Not only do I get to spend quality time with friends and mentors on the course but I also get to meet new people of the same caliber. Some of the introductions made on the green have led to new business opportunities.

I get that, sometimes, it's a financial stretch to get into the game, much less choose your seat, but here's the truth: If money is the reason you think you can't do something to change your life, then money is the reason you need to do whatever it takes to change your life.

Several years back, I had hit a milestone in my business and earned the opportunity to go to a major event in Singapore. The only problem was that, between the tickets, airfare, and five nights at the Marina Bay Sands, it was going to cost me $7,500, and that was a major stretch for me at the time. Qualifying for the event was a huge deal for me. It was a cross between a celebration, world-class training, and networking with incredibly successful businesspeople, and I almost didn't go because I thought I couldn't afford it.

The deadline to register was coming up when a buddy (who already had his ticket) called and asked if I'd made my reservations yet. When I told him I wasn't planning on going, he couldn't believe it. "Dude, you have got to go!" he said. "You don't want to be sitting at home watching videos of all of us in Singapore, knowing you could have been there." Then he reminded me what I already knew to be true: "The fact you're thinking about not going because of finances is exactly why you need to be there."

I knew he was right, so I made it happen

I'd had to work hard to qualify for a seat in the *back* of the room for that event, but it didn't' matter. I was *in the room*. Being there set some pretty incredible opportunities into motion that I would have missed out on otherwise. It was at that event I met one of my best friends and mentors. It's also where I met Mark Lachance, who later invited me to speak to his team and inspired me to write this book.

Bottom line: Even if you can't choose your seat, get in the room! Find or create opportunities to be around the kind of people you want to be like or do business with. Getting in the room is the most important thing. If you can't afford a ticket, be a waiter or work at the book table. Do what you need to do to get in the room. What you see and hear from the people there will inspire you and boost your confidence, and you just may meet your next business partner.

What's Your Code?

What do you **believe** about yourself? Are you worthy of achieving great things? Are you stuck in a comparison trap?

What habits would help you **become** the best, most confident version of yourself?

Does your current **behavior** support your beliefs and desires for your future?

Based on the answer above, does that behavior **belong** in your code?

Chapter 7
ESSENTIAL 5
ACTION

*Inaction breeds doubt and fear. Action breeds confidence
and courage. If you want to conquer fear, do not sit home
and think about it. Go out and get busy.*

—Dale Carnegie

A SPLIT-SECOND ACTION can change everything.

On a flight to Long Beach, California, for a wedding
a while back, an older gentleman passed me on the way to
the restroom. He struggled with the door until an attendant
stepped out from the galley to help him.

I was sitting on the front row in 1C, watching *12 Mighty
Orphans*, and had almost forgotten he was in there when he
opened the door. I glanced up, surprised, and immediately
noticed how pale he looked. *Something's not right*, I thought.

He stood at the folding door a few seconds, as if he were trying to get his balance, and then took a slow, wobbly step in my direction. The next step was even more wobbly. And then I noticed his eyes as they rolled up and back. I knew he was going down.

Without thinking, I leaped from my chair and caught him as he fainted and fell, dead weight, into my arms.

I didn't have to stand there holding him for long. The flight attendant who had been sitting in the folding seat near the cockpit door jumped up and helped me ease him down into her chair as he came to again. When another flight attendant joined her to help take care of him, I returned to my seat.

A few minutes later, a guy, whose seat was across the aisle from where the older gentleman had been sitting, tapped me on the shoulder. "I told the flight attendant something wasn't right with that old guy," he said. "I knew he needed help, but she just ignored me... and him." His tone made it clear he was annoyed the attendant hadn't taken action. "I'm glad you were there to catch him," he said.

Later, when the gentleman finally made his way back to his seat, this time flanked by an attendant, he paused as he passed me. "Thanks for your help," he said.

"Of course," I replied. He looked pale and feeble. "I hope you're feeling better."

I turned and watched him take his seat, and all I could think was, *What if I hadn't acted quickly enough?* He could have bashed his head on the wall, seats, or floor going down—maybe all three.

If I learned anything from that flight, it was not to ignore the instinct to act. As I've thought more about that lesson, I have realized it's way too easy to dismiss the urge to do something—*anything*—when fear or self-doubt is involved or even when personal comfort is at risk. That's true in extreme scenarios as well as in our day-to-day lives.

You may remember the news reports of passengers failing to act when a woman was raped on a commuter train in Philadelphia in October 2021. A few witnesses filmed the crime, but no one stepped in and tried to help the woman during the attack. Finally, an off-duty transit employee walked by and immediately reported the disturbing scene. Three minutes after that report, the train stopped, and police boarded the train and pulled the assailant off the victim. The whole encounter, according to surveillance cameras, lasted forty minutes. For thirty-seven of those minutes, *no one* did anything to help. No one tried to stop the rapist. No one called 911.

That's an extreme example of inaction that, if we give people the benefit of the doubt, was probably the result of fear or the "bystander effect," which is what happens when witnesses don't intervene when others are present. Everyone assumes someone else will help, so no one does.

(By the way, this is why first-aid trainers teach people not to say, "*Somebody* help," during an emergency. *Somebody*, too many times, is equivalent to *nobody*. If you need someone to do something, like call 911, for example, look a specific person in the eyes and say, "*You* call 911.")

More common scenarios of inaction, while far less extreme than that occurrence on the train, can threaten personal success on any number of levels. Fear and lack of belief can keep you from taking the first steps toward greatness, and unwillingness to deal with discomfort will stagnate your potential. That might look like refusing to get out of a warm bed on a cold morning to exercise, choosing not to call customers, or avoiding a difficult conversation with a loved one.

Whether you're dealing with an extreme scenario or an everyday decision, my hope is your code of behavior will include immediate *action* on your part. Be the one who takes a risk, moves to action, or simply dials 911 if the situation warrants it. Be the one who moves with deliberate discipline every day toward your goals.

Even if the action seems small, do it. Why? Because how you do anything is how you do everything. If you're not willing to act on the small things, you won't be prepared to move when big challenges and opportunities come your way.

Show up with excellence. Do the small things *now*. That's how you build your health, your wealth, your character, your integrity, and your success.

The cure for disbelief and fear is action. Don't let inaction kill your dreams.

Procrastination Lies

If more information was the answer, then we'd all be billionaires with perfect abs.

—Derek Sivers

You have your goal.

You know your why.

You have identified what you need to do to accomplish that goal. And you know who you need to become to make your goal a reality.

Now it's time for action. This is where the rubber meets the road. The longer you wait to act, the less likely it is you will ever take the first step. That's the deadly truth about procrastination.

So why do we procrastinate? One interesting study from researchers at The University of Sheffield revealed people most commonly use this self-defeating tactic to regulate their moods or emotions. In other words, we procrastinate because we want to feel good in the moment. The problem is our inaction inevitably backfires and makes us feel worse about ourselves, which makes us even less likely to take action. It's a vicious cycle that, if perpetuated long enough, can lead to chronic stress, depression, and anxiety and can manifest in physical ways, including chronic illness and heart disease.

The solution is to break the procrastination cycle. One way to do that is to be self-aware enough to recognize the lies that lead us to put off until someday (in other words, *never*) what we should do today. Are you telling yourself any of these lies?

Lie: I need more information. Doesn't that sound like a logical excuse for delaying action? Education is a good thing, right? Yes. I'm a huge proponent of continuing education and professional development. The lie is that you need to have *all* the information before you get started. Don't be so busy getting prepared that you never get started.

The world is addicted to information. A study by Loup Funds, a research-based investment firm, noted that "the average global consumer spends eighty-two hours per week consuming information." That adds up to approximately 69 percent of our waking hours. Just imagine what you could accomplish with even half of those hours devoted to actually *doing* the thing you say you want to do.

Truth: You already have more information than you need to take the first step. Fear of looking or feeling stupid or incapable is more likely the real reason you're putting off the task. You can get whatever information you really need by using the smartphone you carry in your pocket, either to look it up or to reach out to a mentor for on-the-go advice.

Lie: I need to (fill in the blank) first. This procrastination tactic is tricky because you *feel* productive when you walk the dog, check your email, or phone a friend. The problem is none of those activities are going to move you closer to accomplishing your goal. And chances are, none of those excuses are the real reason you're procrastinating. When an "urgent" reason to skip out on productive action pops up, ask yourself what else is going on. Are you feeling fearful you don't have what it takes to succeed? Do you worry you aren't smart or good enough to pull off your goal? Are you afraid of trying and failing?

Truth: You need to be self-aware enough to prioritize goal-getting actions. Yes, you need to walk the dog. Just don't use that poor animal as an excuse. Be honest with yourself about what's really important. Decide you're strong enough, brave enough, and disciplined enough to do the right thing. Jim Rohn offered this advice: "Don't start your day until you have it finished on paper first." Make a plan for your time and stick to it. Success builds. Small wins matter because they move you toward your goal *and* because your confidence grows as you get results. Figure out what you need to do in a given day and be disciplined about making it happen. No excuses. Not even the dog.

Lie: It will take too long. All the tasks involved with big goals can seem overwhelming. Whether you're looking at a year-long plan to get fit, a five-year plan to build a business, or a ten-year plan to put $1 million in your retirement account, if you're like most people, the wait seems too long. As a culture, we are impatient. We want instant results *now*. So we put off starting, and the delay costs us our dreams.

Truth: If you don't start now, you will regret it. Success starts the moment you do. As the saying goes, "Most people overestimate what they can do in one year and underestimate what they can do in five or ten years."

Overestimating your short-term results sets you up for disappointment. If you expect to see major changes in your physique after one workout or one week of healthy eating, you'll be likely to give up on week two. So even as you stretch your goals beyond what others may consider realistic, set reasonable expectations for your short term results. Go back to the action plan you developed in Essential 1 when you set your goal and determined what markers would most effectively measure progress. You might, for example, set an interim endurance or a weightlifting goal rather than watch the scale. For a business goal, give yourself monthly—or even daily—challenges to achieve. For a financial goal, you might start by setting investment goals for each month rather than waiting for your portfolio to creep slowly upward.

In a year, you could be stronger and leaner—or not. In five years, you could have a thriving business—or not. In ten years (or less!), you could have $1 million in your checking or retirement account—or not. The same amount of time will pass regardless of your actions—the difference will be your results.

It is possible to end the self-defeating cycle of procrastination, and you can start by owning up to the real reasons you aren't doing what you know you need to do. **Execution and procrastination are both choices! One leads to greatness. One halts your greatness**.

What are you waiting for?

Recognize the Rewards of Action

Great things never came from comfort zones.

—Neil Strauss

Procrastination is a bad short-term solution to feeling good *right now*. Research shows it's less of a time-management issue and more of an emotional-management issue. Ending procrastination requires not only action but also a shift in mindset.

Humans have the tendency to kick themselves when they're down. I can't believe I did that again.

I'm so stupid.

I'm lazy.

I'm never going to succeed.

What do you tell yourself when you screw up? Chances are, you talk to yourself way more harshly than you would a friend. (And if you do, chances are you won't keep those friends for long.)

Be careful about negative self-talk. Your words are powerful, and your mind will believe what you tell it.

You've heard the metaphor about the carrot and the stick. You can beat a donkey with a stick, trying to get it to move, and the only thing you'll get is tired. That donkey isn't going to move just because you want it to! But if you tie a carrot to the end of that stick and hold it out in front of the donkey, it will happily move toward that tasty-looking reward.

So, yeah, if we connect this metaphor back to your tendency (or mine) to beat ourselves up when we procrastinate, you're an ass. Don't worry—so am I. But we can change that!

Negative reinforcement can be effective in extreme cases (e.g., rational people don't commit murder because they want to avoid jail), but research shows it's less effective when it comes to overcoming procrastination or reaching goals. Beating yourself up or even focusing on the negative consequences of inaction rarely inspires us to get up and get to work.

Unfortunately, putting the carrot one year, five years, or ten years into the future isn't all that effective either. Knowing a reward is waiting for your future self doesn't really matter to your present self. Your present self doesn't care that your future self is going to be healthy and strong if you eat right and exercise today. Your present self wants to binge Netflix and eat a whole pizza.

The solution is to reward yourself way before you reach that long-term goal. Even something as simple as noticing how good you feel after working out can be enough to help develop a habit of regular exercise, for example. A little bit of personal acknowledgment or celebration for what you did today will make you want to repeat that action tomorrow. *Remember how good it felt when you were done? Get your ass out the door so you can feel like that again.*

Acknowledge your progress and celebrate your success. Let yourself revel for a few minutes in your accomplishments so your mind can appreciate the fact that there's more on the horizon when you take the right actions. Celebrating the little victories now paves the way for greater success. Repeat your small wins often enough, and you'll look back a year from now and be shocked at how far you've come.

Work for It, Don't Photoshop It!

Everybody wants to be famous, but nobody wants to do the work. I live by that. You grind hard so you can play hard. At the end of the day, you put all the work in, and eventually, it'll pay off. It could be in a year; it could be in thirty years. Eventually, your hard work will pay off.

—Kevin Hart

Everything you do affects everything you become. That's the bottom-line truth about your code of behavior. When you take action toward your goals and start seeing results, your confidence will increase, which improves your discipline, which feeds into more focused action. It's a self-perpetuating cycle of growth.

My dream for building a business started because I was sick and tired of being broke, bored, and generally dissatisfied. I set my first few business goals with the desire to get out of that life. For me, that meant setting goals that enabled me to get profitable fast. At first, I wasn't focused on a six- or seven-figure income.

I didn't know much then about setting SMART goals, so I didn't even have a number on my dream yet. My goal was simple: Stop feeling broke! I was sick and tired of living paycheck to paycheck and having to budget every dollar. I knew, though, I could create a better life and income for myself as an entrepreneur because I was in charge of my earning potential. If I would actually put in the work, I would reap the rewards because I was building *my* dream—not working for someone else's dream.

I also knew I would have to hustle to make it happen.

Realizing it would be way too easy to get distracted by the party scene, I changed my environment. I intentionally spent more time with people who supported me in my efforts and challenged me to do more—and less time with people who told me I was stupid for even trying to change my life. Hanging out with entrepreneurs like Tim, who had done what I wanted to do, inspired me to keep going. They showed me it could be done, how to do it, and that I could do it. Tim's conviction, not only in his dreams but in what was possible for *me*, lit a fire in me. He believed in me and wanted me to succeed. He saw in me what I wasn't able to see or believe about myself yet, which made me want to work even harder to prove him right. I borrowed his belief until my discipline and confidence had fully kicked in.

Goals, desire, discipline, and confidence. All of those things were essential to the code of behavior I was developing for my new life, but none of them would have gotten me very far without the fifth essential: *action*. I had to work for my success. So do you.

Growing up, I developed a mindset of expectation: I expected a boss would give me a job and pay me well. Even though I was willing to work, I basically had a handout mindset. I mistakenly made my welfare someone else's responsibility. Being around other goal-driven, disciplined, confident people completely changed my mindset. I watched and followed not only their examples but also adopted their philosophy that every person is in charge of, in control of, and responsible for their own success. They didn't wait around for a boss or supervisor to tell them what to do. They set incredible goals for themselves, devised a plan of action, and then *did the work* to make those goals a reality.

One of the secrets to success is simply to do what successful people do. (It sounds simple, doesn't it? That's because it is.)

That's what I did, and my mindset shifted from one of feeling like the world owed me something to I owe myself the best.

Look around. What's working for the most successful people you've chosen to be in your circle of influence? How did they get there? Was it legal, ethical, and moral? If the answer to those questions is yes, the next thing you have to ask yourself is, *Am I willing to do the work to get where they are and have what they have?*

Tim got up early every day and got to work. When I lived with him, I did the same. (I had no choice. If I wasn't up, he would come banging on the door and wake me up!) He set daily goals and crushed them. I did too. The more productive I was, the better my results. The better my results, the more I *wanted* to work, and the more I wanted to achieve. It was like Kevin Hart's metaphor of the game. Every level of success I reached opened up another door of possibility. I became addicted to success! At ten o'clock at night, my mind would be spinning with ideas to try. My goals didn't care if I was tired. I was inspired!

In Essential 1: Goals, I mentioned Grant Cardone's book *The 10X Rule*. The core idea of Cardone's message is that to attain lasting and ongoing success, you have to dream big—huge. His advice is to multiply whatever your goal is by a factor of ten and then do ten times the work you think would be necessary to achieve that goal.

Most people, Cardone points out, do one or the other. Some people set huge goals but fail to put in the necessary work, so they never get what they say they want. Without a 10X plan of action to achieve their huge goals, they simply don't work hard enough for it.

Other people work like crazy but never get their mindset right. They put in the hours, and they have killer work ethics, but they can't see themselves as wildly successful. Even if they've got the hustle, they end up losing whatever it is they worked so hard to achieve because they don't believe they are worthy of it.

But do I really have to 10X my effort? Is that really worth it? If that's what you're thinking, consider this: If you limit your goals, you restrict your potential for success. You may achieve what you set out to, but the results may leave you feeling discouraged. Huge goals that require mega hustle yield huge returns, and they are more likely to last. Beyond their staying power, those huge results tend to spur even bigger dreams and stronger desires. Is it gonna take work? You bet. But hell yeah, it's worth it!

People who take massive levels of action and experience massive success don't tell you to slow down. It's only the ones not doing much or just enough to get by that bring up slowing down. If someone is telling you your goal is too big or that you're working too hard, you can bet they haven't experienced this 10X factor in their lives. They've worked and achieved just enough to feel the pain without enjoying the full benefits they could have had if they had pushed the limits of their belief and effort. "Talk to anyone who is wildly, extraordinarily successful in some field, and they will tell you it never felt like work," Cardone says. "It feels like work to most people because the payoff is not substantial enough and doesn't yield an adequate victory to feel like something that isn't 'work.'"

Remember 100/0. Take 100 percent responsibility for everywhere you are and everywhere you're not and make zero excuses. Whatever your dream is, be willing to work for it. We live in a world made shiny by filters and Photoshop. The norm is to cut corners and complain that life isn't going as planned.

In the gym, my motto is *Don't Photoshop it! Work for it!* That message applies to abs and asses, but it also applies to anything else you want to achieve or acquire. Develop a next-level work ethic, and make it happen. There are those who want success, and there are those who work for it. Be one of the few who is willing to work for it. Your dreams are worth it. *You* are worth it.

Don't Stop

> *Let's not get tired of doing what is good. At just the right time, we will reap a harvest of blessing if we don't give up.*
>
> **—The Apostle Paul,** Galatians 6:9, NLT

While you're out there hustling your hardest, there will come a day when life knocks you to the ground. I've had plenty of those days, but the one that hit the hardest was December 26, 2019. That's the day I got the call that my little brother, Jacob, had died from a drug overdose. It's hard to express the pain of that crushing blow and all the thoughts that trampled me in the days and weeks that followed.

I'd seen him a few weeks prior to his death, and I knew something wasn't right with him. He was living with his dad at the time. When my mom or I would ask him what was going on, he would just blame his kidney dialysis for the fact that he looked like shit. When he got into a really bad wreck about a month before his death, he told us he had fallen asleep while driving. He was just tired.

It was all a lie.

Mom reached out to her ex-husband (Jacob's father) about him, but he blew off her concern saying, "Aw, he's fine," but we knew that didn't feel true. After his death, I learned our mom had suspected he was using drugs again. Trying to save him from himself, she even offered to have him live with her—as long as he would submit to drug tests. He refused the offer.

My brother was an adult. He made his own choices, just like I'd done. But still, I felt bad for him. A few years prior to all this, he had developed kidney issues, and my mom donated a kidney to save him. He was good to go, medically speaking. To deal with the pain of recovery, the doctor prescribed him hydrocodone. You've heard about the opioid crisis, right? My family knows about it all too well, unfortunately. He ended up getting addicted to pain killers.

We thought he had beaten his addiction, but we were wrong.

Not a day goes by that I don't miss him. I still feel his presence and talk to him. I wish I could see him again, talk with him, take him to dinner, listen to him sing and play the guitar again. But I can't. We'll never get the chance to do those things again—at least not in this life. Jacob's death feels like such an unnecessary, senseless loss. There are days when I wonder what I could have done to prevent it. The "what if" game is a dangerous one, and if I'm not careful, those days suck me into the darkness.

Thankfully, it's true that "even the darkest night will end, and the sun will rise."

Pain and struggle are part of life. No one is immune to suffering or heartbreak. Everyone gets knocked down.

You have to get back up. It hurts, and the hit doesn't get easier, but you get stronger.

Losing Jacob is one of the things that started waking me up to just how precious life is. The pain my family and I experienced because of his death made me want to do whatever it takes to be there for my family—to love them better and to take care of them. The whole experience of recovering from that kind of blow has made me more empathetic to what others are dealing with and more convinced than ever that my purpose is to help others thrive.

Maybe you've been knocked down before and are afraid of taking another hit like that. I hear ya. I don't want that for you either. What I really don't want, though, is for you to miss out on all your life could be.

Don't quit.

Get up and take the next small step toward greatness.

What's Your Code?

What do you **believe** about your current level of activity? Is it enough to get you where you want to go? Do you need to double, triple, or even 10X your effort?

What would your code need to look like for you to **become** ten times more successful than you are right now?

Does your current **behavior** support that target?

Based on the answer above, what behaviors **belong** in your code?

Chapter 8
THE CHOICE IS YOURS

There is no excuse for not living up to your
fullest potential. No excuse.

—Eric Thomas

Eric Thomas was born to a single teenage mother. His father ghosted them both. For years, though, he didn't know that part of the story. When he was a teenager, he learned that the man he thought was his father wasn't his biological dad. The news turned what had been a pretty happy childhood upside down. It rocked his world—destroying his self-belief and coloring his attitude toward everyone and everything—to think his mother had him by accident. He gave up on school, rejected all authority, and eventually—after a family argument one day—left home.

Eric dropped out of school at sixteen and ended up living on the streets of Detroit. "I ate out of trash cans," he said. "I slept in abandoned buildings." To say his life was hard doesn't scratch the surface of his reality as a young, homeless African American male in one of the United States' most dangerous cities.

Things changed for Thomas, though, when a preacher he met on the street one day offered him the gift of hope. "He really just spoke life into me at a time when I was lost," Thomas explained during a magazine interview. "He told me I had an untapped gift that, if tapped into, would save lives!"

The preacher convinced him there was more for him than the life he was living. Holding on to that belief, Thomas found work waiting tables and earned his GED. He went to college in Huntsville, Alabama, on a part-time basis. The road was long, but he was determined not to give up. In 2001, twelve years later, he earned his bachelor's degree.

He didn't wait until he had completed his undergraduate degree to start making a difference in people's lives. As an undergrad student, he and a group of guys started a program to help others earn their GEDs. He also surrounded him-self with people who inspired him, working with a group called WSB: Willing, Successful, and Black. The positive, forward-thinking he saw in action with WSB opened a new world to him, and it was because he connected with this group that he became a speaker.

"One day, one of the guys didn't show up to speak," he says. "I was there, so I had to do it." On the fly and without notes, Eric spoke from the heart. His message resonated with the audience—and lit a new passion for him. He couldn't wait for the next opportunity—and then the next. "Each time I would speak, I would feel superhuman. I knew at nineteen years old that this was a gift, something special, and that public speaking was what I was going to do as my hustle."

On a mission to inspire, he became known as ET, The Hip Hop Preacher and began a career as a motivational speaker, author, and coach. Thomas went on to earn a master's in educational leadership and a doctorate in education administration from Michigan State University and has never stopped empowering others to see the potential within themselves.

Today, Thomas, who is one of my favorite people on the planet (I listen to his videos almost daily), continues to speak from the heart. He is a talented and well-paid keynote speaker, who travels the world, bringing a no-holds-barred message of possibility and personal responsibility to school kids, prisoners, collegiate and professional sports teams, and business leaders alike. He's a four-time author, successful business owner, and the host of the popular *Secrets to Success* podcast.

Thomas's life has come a long way from the streets of Detroit. He's a loving husband and father, and he has impacted countless lives with his message of hope. As he speaks to audiences, he points out it wasn't his circumstances that changed him—*he* changed his circumstances. His life didn't get better until he made a choice: "I changed," he says. "I stopped being the victim. I stopped saying, 'I've gotta wait for good things to happen to me,' and I said, 'I'm going to grind. I'm going to fight. I'm going to work. I'm going to press toward. I'm going to learn. Every single day, I'm going to do everything in my power to become a victor and not a victim.'"

Are You Choosing Victory or Defeat?

> *No one may achieve success without first knowing precisely what he wants.*
>
> **—Napoleon Hill**

Your circumstances might not be so desperate that you're homeless, living on the streets, or eating out of trashcans. But there is something in your life you know you want to change—or *need* to change. Maybe it's a broken relationship you need to repair or a toxic one you need to leave. Maybe you hate your job or are living paycheck to paycheck. Maybe you're extremely overweight, and your health is in the gutter. Maybe you're like I was, and you're dealing with substance addiction. Whatever is holding you back from living your best possible life, *you* have to make a choice: Are you going to be a victor or a victim?

The ability to choose to dramatically change our lives is what separates us from every other life-form. We have the power to consider our options. We have the capacity to consider potential outcomes, weigh our chances for success or failure, and even create new options if we don't like the ones on the table. We have the power to choose to change our thoughts from negative to positive. And we have the choice to live with gratitude each day for a heart that's still beating and the potential not just to survive but to *thrive.*

Your code of behavior—the dreams, mindsets, and actions that make or break your success—consists of your day-by-day, minute-by-minute choices. So what's your choice? Victim or victor?

You've hung in here this long, so my hope and belief for you is you're choosing victory over defeat. You know what you want, you've identified the code of behavior that will get you there, and you're willing to work for it. That's awesome!

As Zig Ziglar said, "You don't have to be great to start, but you have to start to be great." Making the decision to choose victory and *work* for it is your first step to greatness. And, *yes*, you have it in you to be great and to live with excellence. But I wouldn't be doing you a favor if I led you to believe everything is going to be easy from here on out.

Even with a clear code of behavior to direct you, the truth is there will be obstacles and setbacks. You will be tempted to give up or give in. Sometimes you will feel like you're under attack—because you *are*.

Anytime you decide you're going to do great things so you can make this world a better place, you will run up against opposition. In one of my all-time favorite books, *Outwitting the Devil*, Napoleon Hill explains this persistent, devilish opposition—both internal and external—is always there, trying to lure us off our chosen paths. To overcome opposition, you and I have to wake up and say, "The devil's not gonna beat me today!" Each step forward requires our focused desire and the discipline to choose which thoughts we will allow in our minds and which habits will shape our lives. Every day we must battle against fear, self-doubt, and the reluctance to leave our comfort zones. To win the battle and ultimately experience endless victory, we have to live with extreme inspiration and unlimited confidence.

Extreme Inspiration

The swiftest way to triple your success is to double your investment in personal development.

—Robin Sharma

When I speak to audiences, the energy in the room is off the charts. I'm talking about business and expanding personal potential, but the vibe in the room is anything but boring. People are excited! After speaking, I always enjoy meeting people in the crowd. We take selfies, and they tell me about their dreams and what they're going to do when they get home. I always invite people to stay in touch and let me know when they hit their goals.

A few people take me up on that offer. I love seeing the pictures and notes they send in celebration of their achievements. Their excitement and accomplishments energize me!

Most people, though, I never hear from again. Or if I do, it's at another event months or years later, where they tell me they haven't gotten as far as they wanted. They got excited about their goals and made a plan, and then life got in the way. It doesn't matter what excuses they offer because *all* excuses equate to a lack of action or persistence. Even though their reasons and excuses vary, the outcome is the same: Those people are still stuck in the same place in their lives as they were the last time we talked.

What's the difference between the achievers and those who are stuck?

Inspiration.

One person stays motivated and completes the mission. The other one's motivation dies, right along with their dreams. Inspiration—that internal driving desire—is the force that keeps them focused and moving forward.

When you go to a great seminar, you get inspired by the speaker's story and excitement for life. When you listen to a powerful podcast about people overcoming odds or doing amazing things with their lives, you get inspired by their accomplishments. When you read a book like this one, you feel inspired to believe anything is possible for you.

All that inspiration motivates you to set a purposeful goal and move toward it step-by-step with confidence. At first, nothing can take you off course. You're on fire! Focused on your target, you do the work, and, little by little, you start seeing the results you want.

Inspiration is important. It's powerful and necessary for a great life. But inspiration will only get you so far.

At some point, the shine wears off. Enough hits, bad days, or rejections in a row throws a cold bucket of water on the fire of motivation that inspiration lit. Embers turn to soggy ash, and, sooner or later, you decide to take a day off—or a week, maybe even a month or a year—from living by the code of behavior you've designed for your life.

Inspiration is external. It's what happens *to* you.

Motivation is what you *do* with inspiration.

Extreme inspiration leads to extreme motivation, which is what empowers you to stay focused and committed to your dreams when times get tough. You're going to need extreme inspiration because life is not always sunshine and rainbows. How are you going to stay motivated when you get fired from your job? How will you stay motivated when you didn't get the job you wanted, when your business fails, or when a relationship falls apart? How will you stay motivated when you reach a level of success you've never had before and start to feel comfortable, even though you haven't reached your ultimate goal?

If you don't have a continual flow of inspiration, you'll be more likely to quit or give up when you face challenges. You'll also be more likely to get complacent and be tempted to coast when things are going well enough.

Extreme inspiration is *intentional* inspiration. It's what you need to stay motivated when what you *really* want to do is slide back into the comfort of old habits. Your outer life always reflects your inner life, so you've got to take care of your mindset and stay positive regardless of what's going on around you.

Extreme inspiration means you keep pouring positive messages, purpose, and belief into your mind with the things you listen to and read. What you feed your mind—whether that's through song lyrics, personal development books like this one, mentoring and coaching programs like those I offer my clients, as well as seminars, podcasts, or even what you hear from the people you spend the most time with—can build you up and keep you strong.

I'd love to work with you. Scan the QR code to learn more about my Code of Behavior Coaching Program

The wrong kinds of input, however, will tear you down. Good stuff in. Good stuff out.

Bad stuff in. Bad stuff out.

Nothing in. Nothing out—at least not enough to keep you motivated.

You get to choose what goes into your mind, so choose wisely. My hope is you'll be extremely inspired by this book. But understand it's up to you to turn that inspiration into the kind of motivation that moves you to action. Start by creating and then maintaining the right conditions for success.

Create the Mental and Physical Conditions for Success

People often say that motivation doesn't last. Well, neither does bathing—that's why we recommend it daily.

—*Zig Ziglar*

Great sequoias are the largest trees in the world. *Extreme* is the right word for these massive trees. But they don't start out great, and their life can't even begin without struggle. Sequoias need the intense heat of a fire to release their seeds. Without the devastation of a forest fire, existing trees will keep growing, but no new ones can grow. The heat rising up from the flames dries out the sequoia cones and causes them to open. A couple of weeks after the fire passes, the seeds fall from the cones to the charred ground below.

Those seeds? They are the size of a grain of oatmeal. *Tiny.*

They take root in the dark earth and get their nutrients from sunlight, rain, and the ground itself. Without any one of those things, the tree can't grow. But with the right amount of each, they thrive.

We are similar to those trees. If we don't have the right conditions, we can't thrive. Our environment, inputs, habits, mindset, and relationships are all part of the conditions that determine whether we thrive or die.

The trouble is, we don't like the fires of challenge. The work and struggle of success requires daily effort and growth. Without a clear code of behavior supported by each of the five essentials, it is easy to give up and revert to behaviors that seem, at least temporarily, easier and more comfortable.

The question is, how do we protect or prevent ourselves from going back to those places?

One-and-done inspiration isn't going to last long term. You need extreme inspiration to stay motivated, which means you have to continually feed your mind and create the conditions that help you stay positive, focused, and on track to becoming your best.

When I feel myself slipping back into behaviors or mindsets that don't belong in my code—skipping workouts, overindulging, avoiding calls, comparing myself to others—it's usually because I'm not taking time to do the mental work I need to do to stay sharp.

If I'm not doing my personal development every day, the little things start to bother me. But when I work at keeping my mind sharp and my body strong, nothing can faze me. It doesn't matter what life throws at me. I'm going to stay positive. I have to choose *daily* to live out of faith rather than fear and to get results instead of making excuses.

You have the same choices to make.

I hope you'll make the choice to work on yourself and strengthen your mind *daily*.

Here's what I've learned: It's not what happens to you that breaks you. It's that you aren't mentally prepared.

That's where *extreme inspiration* comes in. Constant attention to your mental sharpness and positive mindset is what prepares you for whatever life throws your way.

To keep yourself from sliding back into behaviors that trap rather than transform you, you must devise a plan for extreme inspiration that will nourish your mind, body, and spirit. Those three aspects of your well-being are crucial. Maintaining level ten excellence in mind, body, and spirit keeps you balanced. But like a tripod, if any one of those aspects is out of whack, the others follow suit—and everything will fall.

Cultivating a positive mindset that empowers you to thrive requires daily effort. I've listed a few ideas below to help you create the mental and physical conditions for success. Do as many of these as you can each day.

- Listen to a positive podcast or an audiobook.

- Read an inspirational or uplifting book for thirty minutes a day.

- Reread your goals and think about why they are important to you.

- Identify one task that will move you closer to a larger goal. Do it!

- Look for the growth opportunity in the middle of difficulty. Rather than running away from a problem, run to them and choose to grow or learn from it.

- Regularly spend time with people who encourage you to be your personal best.

- Before you get out of bed in the morning, say three things you're grateful for.

- Before you go to bed, write down three things that you did well that day.

Don't allow yourself to get complacent when it comes to strengthening your mindset and resolve. You're either growing or dying, so commit to yourself—or, better yet, to an accountability partner—to doing the mental work daily to stay inspired and keep growing!

Make Yourself Accountable

Accountability breeds response-ability.

—*Stephen Covey*

I'm always competing.

I compete against myself, always trying to do more reps, more weight, and better deals than I did yesterday, last month, or last year.

When I have kids, I'm not going to be the kind of dad who lets them win at Candy Land. (Some people might not agree with me on this, but that's okay.) It's just not in me to play at less than my best.

Competition makes life fun for me. Whether it's a round of golf or a game of basketball, I enjoy competing with others because it pushes me to strive for excellence.

The same is true for me in business. I'm part of an entrepreneur networking mastermind group in which everyone works in a different industry. Part of the challenge and fun of being in this mastermind is that we each encourage the others constantly to level up.

Working alongside people pushes you mentally to go faster and further than you would on your own. It's true regardless of the goal. There's something motivating about competing *together*. Competitive accountability is not about comparing yourself to those you're working with or who are running beside you. It's about spurring one another on and bringing out the best in yourself and those around you. It creates a level of accountability we rarely maintain when we are working alone.

The idea of being accountable for your personal goals may sound strange if you're not used to checking in with anyone regularly.

What if I fail? What if I want to quit? What if I just don't feel like working?

Well, that's the point. Left to our own devices, it's easy for us to forget or intentionally skip the steps we need to take each day to get to our goals.

Whatever your goal, the truth is, there will be days you don't feel like doing the work. But if you know you'll be checking in with a friend or mentor once a day or once a week and sharing the progress you've made, you're going to want to make sure you have something better to say than, "I didn't feel like working."

Research shows accountability is often the missing ingredient when it comes to following through on a prescribed course of action. Doctors, for example, tell patients to take medication or exercise regularly and come back for a follow-up exam in six months. Much can happen in six months—or nothing can happen. And more often than not, *nothing* is exactly what happens. Doctors assume that because people want to feel better, they will follow their advice.

The reality is that people tend to follow the familiar path of least resistance and end up making no change at all to their daily habits. Five-and-a-half months down the road, the patients may get inspired to try to do something to show progress. Or they just avoid the calls from the doctor's office and skip the next appointment. When regular, weekly check-ins are part of the treatment plan, however, patients make continual progress because they have a plan of action to which they are held accountable.

The bottom line is this: Even when people *want* to change, they need to feel accountable for their progress. That's true in the doctor's office, and it's true when you're striving for any big goal. Accountability is an essential piece of extreme motivation. Find an accountability partner who is brave enough to call you out when you need to be called out and who will encourage you when you need someone to remind you that you *can* achieve the goal you've set for yourself.

One final note: Don't get mad at your accountability partner when they call you out. That's literally their job. It takes courage and genuine care to hold someone accountable. Don't take your accountability partner for granted.

Unlimited Confidence

Confidence comes not from always being right
but from not fearing to be wrong.

—Peter T. McIntyre

Failure isn't the first thing that comes to mind when you think about people who experience exceptional success. Let's face it: They're known for their successes. Failures—even huge failures—tend to get glossed over or forgotten when successes get piled on top of them.

Winston Churchill said, "Success is the ability to go from failure to failure without losing your enthusiasm." That's *unlimited confidence*—knowing, regardless of how many times you fail, what matters is that you continue to get up, pivot, reset, and try again.

That's a lesson Jon Favreau seems to have learned in his career in the film industry. Favreau is a writer, producer, actor, and director (sometimes playing all of those roles on a single project). He has worked on hundreds of popular movies and television shows, ranging from Marvel's *Iron*

Man and *Avengers* series to the football classic *Rudy* to the live-action reboots of *The Lion King* and *The Jungle Book* to *The Sopranos, Elf,* and *Chef.*

The diversity of his projects shows a willingness to take risks and constantly expand his skills. Not all of his films have been immediate box office hits. Some, like *Rudy* (his first character role in a film), flopped at the box office but gained a following over time. Others like *Zathura* and *Cowboys and Aliens* (both of which he directed and produced) never fully connected with audiences. The blockbuster Marvel movies rake in massive ticket sales but get plenty of criticism from filmmakers, including a couple of Favreau's heroes, Martin Scorsese and Francis Ford Coppola. These two directors have publicly criticized his work, saying superhero movies aren't "real cinema" but rather are "despicable."

Ouch.

Those risks, failures, and even enduring crappy criticism from people he admires, have paid off over time—in one way or another. "I think you need a healthy amount of failure to grow properly. I wouldn't have developed into who I am today if I hadn't lived through *Zathura* [and] *Cowboys and Aliens,*" Favreau told students at the 2017 Tribeca Film Festival. "People don't understand the rhythm of failure. They don't realize that things may turn out well in the end. Half the success is riding it—not defining yourself one way or the other."

That's good insight for all of us.

It's a common, dangerous mistake to define ourselves by our accomplishments and failures or to confuse our roles with our identities.

Your *identity* is who you are. Your *role* is what you do.

Success and failure, both, are things we experience. They are not who we *are*. Don't confuse your role or experiences with your identity.

The Power of Belief

Whatever the mind can conceive and believe, it can achieve.

—Napoleon Hill

There are two belief mindsets: the belief you *can* and the belief you *can't*. And as Henry Ford famously said, "Whether you believe you can do a thing or not, you are right."

I used to lack belief in myself. I doubted whether I was worth the massive success I wanted. Can you relate?

It doesn't take much for people to stop believing in themselves. A simple, thoughtless comment from a teacher, parent, stepparent, or friend can make children second-guess themselves. Enough failures or rejections can make anyone want to give up (which is why we need extreme inspiration).

If you doubt yourself and your ability to succeed, I have good news for you: Belief is a skill you can learn. Unlimited confidence is a trait you can develop.

Everyone experiences self-doubt from time to time. The difference between those who break the chains of doubt and those who remain imprisoned by it is, you guessed it, mindset.

In this book, I've emphasized mindset because it is foundational to each of the five essentials in your code of behavior. Your mindset dictates how big you're willing to dream. Your mindset is a huge factor in your driving motive (your why). Your mindset is what helps you stay keyed in and focused. It's what enables you to believe you *are* worthy of success.

And your mindset determines whether you're going to work for your dreams or give up on them.

Hurt people hurt people. Mark Twain said, "Keep away from people who try to belittle your ambitions. Small people always do that, but the really great make you feel that you, too, can become great." That was definitely true for me. When I changed who I allowed to speak into my life, my mindset changed as well. Once I got out of my own way, *everything* changed for me.

Are you getting in your own way? Be honest with yourself.

Are you sabotaging your success by hanging out with the wrong people? Are you neglecting your mindset or your mental or physical health?

Are you operating at levels of action that are far less than what you're capable of?

If the answer to any of those questions is yes, here's the good news: You can make the decision *right now* to stop those belief-draining, dream-killing behaviors and get out of your own way.

Start by spending time with the right people. They will speak hope to you like that preacher did for Eric Thomas or motivational speaker Earl Shoaff did for Jim Rohn. The right people will let you borrow their belief in you until you find your own, like my mentor Tim did for me. The right people will encourage you. Like a good coach, they'll kick your ass if you need it—or tell you to take a break and regroup and try again.

If you're surrounded by people who belittle your ambitions, remember it's okay to take a break from them and love them from a distance. If you don't have someone who is speaking hope and encouragement into your life, let me be that person for you. Borrow my belief in you until you find your own.

Believing you *can* win is the first stepping-stone to success.

Believe in yourself. You were born with greatness inside of you, so act like it! Go show the world what you are made of.

Believe good things can happen for you. You have the power to create the conditions for amazing opportunities to find you.

Believe you're worth it. You're worthy of your best possible life.

Believe your past doesn't have to determine your future. What matters is what you do with this moment.

Believe you matter. You were created with and designed for a purpose.

Endless Victory

Begin with the end in mind.

—Stephen Covey

The power of belief is that, with it, you can experience end-less victory. You can accomplish whatever you set your mind to. If you truly focus your energy—your effort, time, and thoughts—on what you want to do, have, and be, those things can become your reality.

Focus on winning.

Focus on becoming the best version of yourself. Focus on doing what you were put on this earth to do.

Focus on building the life you truly want. Don't settle for less than that. Put in the work and then expect success.

I had a mentor once call me out on the surprise I would show anytime something good happened to me. (He actually told me I acted like a five-year-old.) He was right. I would say things like, "I can't believe it!" or, "You're never gonna believe what happened!" whenever something great happened.

His point was that success isn't an accident. And it isn't luck or coincidence. It's the result of faith in action, hard work, and intentional choices. Acting surprised, he said, would block more blessings from coming my way because it showed that I thought I didn't deserve the ones I had received.

Now, instead of acting like a five-year-old who just won a year's supply of candy, I say, "Of course that happened!"

That's not bragging or being ungrateful. It's acknowledging that I've done the kind of things that align my life with opportunities for all kinds of good things. I've put in the work, so *of course,* I'm attracting those things into my life.

If you put your focus on winning, you *will* end up winning. It may not happen immediately, but with the right mindset and code of behavior, your success is going to come.

When I look at my life now, I can see one victory after another. Have I fallen down along the way? Of course. Failing is part of getting to success. It's because of my failures that I can relate to people and coach them to experience their own greatness. I've actually been through many of the same challenges they are dealing with. I've done most of it! I made plenty of bad choices. I lived like I was invincible for way too long, and years after the fact, the drug abuse caught up with me, and I ended up flatlining.

Yes, I've failed, but then I learned from it. I've intentionally worked on myself for almost a decade now, shaping my mindset, my actions, my health—my code of behavior. I've conditioned myself and my life to align with the possibility for greatness, for stronger relationships, and for better health and wealth. The victories keep stacking up because I'm operating from the proper code. I'm no longer surprised when good things happen. I *expect* good things to happen because I've put in the work, and I focus on winning.

I hope victory is your focus too. I said earlier that you have a choice between being a victim or a victor—defeat or victory. Here's the thing you need to keep in mind: Victory may not look like victory in the moment.

Victory may look like a failure when actually it's a hard lesson learned. Victory may feel like the end when actually it is a whole new beginning.

Victory may seem disappointing in the short term when actually it's a huge win in the long run.

Many times our victories become our new minimum standards. We never want to go backward, so we set the bar for success even higher the next time.

Don't be shocked if victory doesn't look like what you expect at first. Regardless of the immediate outcome, you win or you learn in the end. Either way, it's a victory.

What's Your Code?

I hope that, as you've read this book, you've taken time to reflect on your code of behavior at the end of each chapter. Flip back through the pages and find your notes. Use this space here to write your code of behavior. Here are some questions to guide you:

What do you **believe** about yourself and your ability to achieve greatness?

What goals, desires, and actions will empower you to **become** who you want to be?

What **behaviors** (habits and daily actions) do you need to do with excellence to live your best life?

What positive mindsets, desires, and relationships **belong** in your code of behavior?

I have the word discipline tattooed on one side of my neck and 100/0 on the other. I see those two reminders every time I look in the mirror. Those tattoos, along with a pair of praying hands that remind me to keep God in the center of my life, sum up my code of behavior. Whatever it takes, I'm committed to doing my best in everything I do and to helping everyone I can. With that in mind, I set my goals and plan my days so that I move forward with excellence. I make time for my most important relationships and consistently take care of my body, mind, and spirit. I expect success and learn from failures. I will not give up. I will not make excuses. I will not quit.

Decide what you want, and then create the code that will empower you to get it. Your code may not look exactly like mine, and that's okay. Your code of behavior doesn't have to be

143

complicated. It just has to be clear and authentic. Remember, the code for the marines is summed up in only two words: Semper Fidelis. That's simple.

And that's the point. Success is simple if you follow the right code.

Update Your Successful Code of Behavior Score

Chapter 9
YOUR NEXT BEST STEP

You are not alone. You are here for a reason.

Two weeks after the heart attack that almost took my life, I stopped in at a tire shop. The place was packed, but before too long, they installed my new wheels. I drove away from the store only to have to turn around and head right back. The wheels were too big and rubbed when I turned the car left or right.

Because of how busy it was, I found myself standing outside and waiting. While I was waiting, a lady walked up to me with a big, nervous smile on her face.

"I'm so glad you came back," she said.

I didn't know the woman or why she cared that I had come back to the store, but she went on to explain.

"When you were here before, I felt like God wanted me to tell you something, and then when you left, I was afraid I had missed my chance."

Now both my curiosity and my guard were up. "Okay," I said, waiting to hear the message.

"I just wanted to let you know that you have a crazy energy about you," she said. "God wanted me to tell you he's watching out for you and that he loves you."

I let her words sink in. Wow! I needed to hear that.

Her statement meant even more because I had flatlined on Easter two weeks prior and walked out of the hospital three days after that—with no damage to my heart and normal pump function.

This lady wasn't walking around the room talking to everyone. As far as I know, she only spoke to me that day because God told her to remind me that he has my back.

The truth is, I believe he has your back too. You're not alone. You are here for a reason.

My hope is, as you've read through this book and developed your personal code of behavior, you've discovered that reason—or at least part of it. If you're anything like me, life will continue to reveal your purpose bit by bit. With every step you take in faith and each word you speak in alignment with who you're destined to become, you'll see that destiny more clearly—because you're creating it.

This is why it's so important for you to wisely create your code of behavior. Every person has a code, but very few people understand that everything flows from this code. If your code permits laziness and dishonesty, this type of negative behavior will result. But if your code demands discipline and integrity, then this type of positive behavior will soon follow.

I've been honored to unpack with you the five essentials to unlocking a life of extreme inspiration, unlimited confidence, and endless victory. I want to congratulate you for finishing the book.

However, we all know books are not meant to simply be read. Rather, they're meant to be applied.

For this reason, I want to invite you to go deeper. On our website (TheCodeOfBehavior.com), you'll find a variety of free tools that will help you do just this, including the Code of Behavior Assessment, bonus videos, and much more.

Perhaps some of you would like to bring the Code of Behavior to your school, organization, or business. If that's the case, please reach out via that same website. We've created a variety of experiences to help you achieve this, including an online course, workshops, and even my keynote speaking availability.

Bottom line, I'm committed to helping you achieve more success. God gave me a second chance for a reason, and one of the main reasons is helping you become all you were created to be.

Remember: You're not alone, and you never will be.

—Jason

BIBLIOGRAPHY

Understanding the Code of Behavior

"Culture & Values." Chick-fil-a.com. Accessed 1/5/2022. https://www.chick-fil-a.com/careers/culture.

Essential 1: Goals

Cardone, Grant. *The 10X Rule: The Only Difference Between Success and Failure*. New York: Wiley, 2011.

Carrey, Jim. "Jim Carrey at MIU: Commencement Address at the 2014 Graduation." May 30, 2014, video, 26:08. https://www.youtube.com/watch?v=V80-gPkpH6M&t=0s.

Gardner, Sarah, and Dave Albee. "Study Focuses on Strategies for Achieving Goals, Resolutions." 2015, press release 266. https://scholar.dominican.edu/news-releases/266.

Essential 2: Desire

Cherry, Kendra. "What Is the Negativity Bias?" VeryWellMind. com. Updated on April 29, 2020. https://www. verywellmind.com/negative-bias-4589618.

Widener, Chris. *Jim Rohn's Eight Best Success Lessons.* United States: Made for Success, 2014.

Essential 3: Discipline

"Bruno Mars: Drug Arrest Was the Reality Check I Needed." *MusicNews.com*, November 21, 2016. https://www. music-news.com/news/UK/101722/Bruno-Mars-Drug-arrest-was-the-reality-check-I-needed

Cardone, Grant. *Be Obsessed or Be Average.* New York: Portfolio. 2016.

Leonhardt, Megan. "Sixty-three percent of Americans Are Living Paycheck to Paycheck Since Covid Hit." *CNBC.com*, December 11, 2020. https://www.cnbc.com/2020/12/11/ majority-of-americans-are-living-paycheck-to-paycheck-since-covid-hit.html.

Logan, Lara. "Bruno Mars on His Artistry: I'm Working Hard for This." *CBS News*, June 11, 2017. https://www. cbsnews.com/news/bruno-mars-on-his-artistry-im-working-hard-for-this/.

Essential 4: Confidence

Canova, Daniel. "Bill Belichick Calls Tom Brady 'The Best Player in NFL History.'" *FoxNews.com*.

February 3, 2022. https://www.foxnews.com/sports/ bill-belichick-calls-tom-brady-best-player-nfl-history.

Guttenkunst, Johannes. *Becoming the GOAT: The Tom Brady Story*. Performed by Charlie Weis, Bill Belichick, Tom Brady, et al., 2021. Little Brother Films/Vision Films. DVD and Blu-ray.

Hart, Kevin. "Life Is a Game." *The Joe Rogan Experience*. https://www.rev.com/blog/transcripts/joe-rogan-kevin-hart-podcast-transcript-may-25-2020.

Kramer, David. *Real World: Timeless Ideas Not Learned in School*. Washington, DC: Rowman & Littlefield Publishers, 2020.

Kryst, Cheslie. "A Pageant Queen Reflects on Turning 30." *Allure.com*. March 4, 2021. https://www.allure.com/story/cheslie-kryst-miss-usa-on-turning-30.

"Tom Brady Biography." *Jockbio.com*. https://web.archive.org/web/20151211062433/http://www.jockbio.com/Bios/BradyTom/Bradybio.html.

"Tom Brady Officially Announces Retirement after 'Thrilling Ride' with Tampa Bay Buccaneers, New England Patriots." *ESPN.com*. February 2, 2022. https://www.espn.com/nfl/story/_/id/33192441/tampa-bay-buccaneers-tom-brady-officially-announces-retirement.

Essential 5: Action

Cardone, Grant. *The 10X Rule: The Only Difference Between Success and Failure*. New York: Wiley, 2011.

Clinton, Doug. "Defining the Future of Human Information Consumption." *Loup Funds*, June 12, 2018. https://loupfunds.com/defining-the-future-of-human-information-consumption/.

Dempsey, Dylan Kai. "Be an Actor and Fail Hard: Jon Favreau's Six Secrets to Being a Great Director." NoFilmSchool.

com, April 28, 2017. https://nofilmschool.com/2017/04/jon-favreau-directors-should-be-actors.

Hill, Napoleon. *Outwitting the Devil: The Secret to Freedom and Success*. Shippensburg, PA: Sound Wisdom, 2021.

Lee, Allen. "Twenty Things You Didn't Know About Eric Thomas." *Money Inc*, 2020. https://moneyinc.com/eric-thomas/.

Oussedik, Elias, et al. "Accountability: A Missing Construct in Models of Adherence Behavior and in Clinical Practice." *Patient Preference and Adherence* vol. 11, #25, July 25, 2017: 1285–1294. doi:10.2147/PPA.S135895. ncbi.nlm.nih.gov/pmc/articles/PMC5536091.

Pockell, Leslie. MBA in a Book: Fundamental Principles of Business, Sales, and Leadership. New York: Grand Central Publishing, 2009.

The Reader's Digest Association. *The Reader's Digest* 51 (September 1947): 64.

Thomas, Eric. "Stop Being a Victim: Eric Thomas About Success." December 3, 2021. *YouTube*, video, 0:51. https://www.youtube.com/watch?v=kdIq4TPSKBY.

Thomas, Eric. "Nothing to Something." *YouTube*, video, May 8, 2013. https://www.youtube.com/watch?v=CocjtcTJaio&ab_channel=etthehiphoppreacher.

Thomas, Eric. "You Owe You." YouTube, video, youtube.com/watch?v=7Oxz060iedY&ab_channel=etthehiphoppreacher.

Rose, Lisa. "Mission Accomplished: The Truth of Eric Thomas," *Empower Magazine*. February 29, 2012. empowermagazine.com/mission-accomplished-the-truth-of-eric-thomas/.

Shoard, Catherine. "Francis Ford Coppola: Scorsese was being kind – Marvel movies are despicable." *The Guardian,* October 21, 2019. theguardian.com/film/2019/oct/21/francis-ford-coppola-scorsese-was-being-kind-marvel-movies-are-despicable.

Ready to Experience
the Full Benefits of this Book?

**Download your FREE Code
of Behavior Bonus Pack**

**Get exclusive access to select videos
and practical templates.**

TheCodeOfBehavior.com/Bonus

**By changing your code of behavior,
you can change your life.**

THE CODE OF BEHAVIOR
BONUS PACK

The Code of Behavior Assessment

Determine your Code of Behavior Score and leverage the power of extreme inspiration, unlimited confidence, and endless victory.

Success doesn't have to be complicated.
All you need is the right Code of Behavior.

TheCodeOfBehavior.com/assessment

THE CODE OF BEHAVIOR
ASSESSMENT

The Code of Behavior Workshop

The Code of Behavior Team Workshop
is a one-of-a-kind experience.
Jason L. Nemes is a master coach and communicator.
He'll help your team achieve better results.
His framework is as easy as A B C:

- **Assess** your team's current code of behavior.
- **Believe** you can change your code.
- **Create** the code that will lead your team to success.

TheCodeOfBehavior.com/workshop

THE CODE OF BEHAVIOR WORKSHOP

Inspire Your Audience
to Take Action

Jason L. Nemes

He'll captivate your audience with his life story and challenge them to make every moment matter. Then, he'll equip them with the know-how to take extreme action and change their code of behavior.

Start the Conversation Today

TheCodeOfBehavior.com/speaker

ABOUT THE AUTHOR

Jason L. Nemes is an international speaker, health and wellness expert, and serial entrepreneur. He attended the University of North Texas where he graduated with a Bachelor Business Administration with an Economics focus. Upon graduating, he sold digital media advertising, but quickly realized this was not his future.

Around that time, Jason encountered an old friend he had repeatedly turned down regarding a business opportunity. This time things were different. Jason saw the success his friend had and decided to go all in as an entrepreneur. He went from holding all his worldly possessions in a trash bag, to becoming a top 1% income earner.

His health and wellness business now generates millions of dollars in sales per year. Known as the "tattedprezzz," he's a top 1% income earner. Although a second heart attack flatlined him on Easter Sunday, April 4, 2021, Jason emerged with an infectious passion for life. Today he inspires and equips clients and audiences to make every moment matter by taking extreme action.

Connect at: JasonLNemes.com